Population Growth

Noah Berlatsky, Book Editor

GREENHAVEN PRESS
A part of Gale, Cengage Learning

GALE
CENGAGE Learning™

Detroit • New York • San Francisco • New Haven, Conn • Waterville, Maine • London

Christine Nasso, *Publisher*
Elizabeth Des Chenes, *Managing Editor*

© 2009 Greenhaven Press, a part of Gale, Cengage Learning

Gale and Greenhaven Press are registered trademarks used herein under license.

For more information, contact:
Greenhaven Press
27500 Drake Rd.
Farmington Hills, MI 48331-3535
Or you can visit our Internet site at gale.cengage.com

For product information and technology assistance, contact us at

Gale Customer Support, 1-800-877-4253
For permission to use material from this text or product, submit all requests online at www.cengage.com/permissions

Further permissions questions can be emailed to permissionrequest@cengage.com

Articles in Greenhaven Press anthologies are often edited for length to meet page requirements. In addition, original titles of these works are changed to clearly present the main thesis and to explicitly indicate the author's opinion. Every effort is made to ensure that Greenhaven Press accurately reflects the original intent of the authors. Every effort has been made to trace the owners of copyrighted material.

Cover image by Peter Parks/AFP/Getty Images.

LIBRARY OF CONGRESS CATALOGING-IN-PUBLICATION DATA

Population growth / Noah Berlatsky, book editor.
        p. cm. -- (Global viewpoints)
    Includes bibliographical references and index.
    ISBN 978-0-7377-4470-5 (hardcover)
    ISBN 978-0-7377-4471-2 (pbk.)
    1. Population. 2. Population--Economic aspects. 3. Population--Environmental aspects. I. Berlatsky, Noah.
    HB871.P6665 2009
    304.6'2--dc22

                                                                2009016635

Printed in the United States of America
1 2 3 4 5 6 7 13 12 11 10 09

Contents

Chapter 1: Population Growth and Hunger

Chapter 2: Population Growth and the Environment

Chapter 3: Population Growth and Economic Development

Chapter 4: Population Growth and Society

Foreword

"The problems of all of humanity can only be solved by all of humanity."
—Swiss author Friedrich Dürrenmatt

Global interdependence has become an undeniable reality. Mass media and technology have increased worldwide access to information and created a society of global citizens. Understanding and navigating this global community is a challenge, requiring a high degree of information literacy and a new level of learning sophistication.

Building on the success of its flagship series, *Opposing Viewpoints*, Greenhaven Press has created the *Global Viewpoints* series to examine a broad range of current, often controversial topics of worldwide importance from a variety of international perspectives. Providing students and other readers with the information they need to explore global connections and think critically about worldwide implications, each *Global Viewpoints* volume offers a panoramic view of a topic of widespread significance.

Drugs, famine, immigration—a broad, international treatment is essential to do justice to social, environmental, health, and political issues such as these. Junior high, high school, and early college students, as well as general readers, can all use *Global Viewpoints* anthologies to discern the complexities relating to each issue. Readers will be able to examine unique national perspectives while, at the same time, appreciating the interconnectedness that global priorities bring to all nations and cultures.

Material in each volume is selected from a diverse range of sources, including journals, magazines, newspapers, nonfiction books, speeches, government documents, pamphlets, organization newsletters, and position papers. *Global Viewpoints* is truly global, with material drawn primarily from international sources available in English and secondarily from U.S. sources with extensive international coverage.

Features of each volume in the *Global Viewpoints* series include:

- An **annotated table of contents** that provides a brief summary of each essay in the volume, including the name of the country or area covered in the essay.

- An **introduction** specific to the volume topic.

- A **world map** to help readers locate the countries or areas covered in the essays.

- For each viewpoint, an **introduction** that contains notes about the author and source of the viewpoint explains why material from the specific country is being presented, summarizes the main points of the viewpoint, and offers three **guided reading questions** to aid in understanding and comprehension.

- **For further discussion** questions that promote critical thinking by asking the reader to compare and contrast aspects of the viewpoints or draw conclusions about perspectives and arguments.

- A worldwide list of **organizations to contact** for readers seeking additional information.

- A **periodical bibliography** for each chapter and a **bibliography of books** on the volume topic to aid in further research.

- A comprehensive **subject index** to offer access to people, places, events, and subjects cited in the text, with the countries covered in the viewpoints highlighted.

Global Viewpoints is designed for a broad spectrum of readers who want to learn more about current events, history, political science, government, international relations, economics, environmental science, world cultures, and sociology—students doing research for class assignments or debates, teachers and faculty seeking to supplement course materials, and others wanting to understand current issues better. By presenting how people in various countries perceive the root causes, current consequences, and proposed solutions to worldwide challenges, *Global Viewpoints* volumes offer readers opportunities to enhance their global awareness and their knowledge of cultures worldwide.

Introduction

> "It's obvious that the key problem facing
> humanity in the coming century is how
> to bring a better quality of life—for 8
> billion or more people—without wreck-
> ing the environment entirely in the at-
> tempt."
>
> Edward O. Wilson,
> as told to Fred Branfman,
> "Living in Shimmering Disequilibrium,"
> Salon.com, April 22, 2000.

Population growth is not a difficult concept; it simply means an increase in the number of people living in a particular place. The ramifications of population growth, how-ever, are extremely controversial. Some people argue that as population grows, more goods are created, and the economy and might of a nation grows as well. As Frederick the Great of Prussia (1712–1786) said, "The number of the people make the wealth of states." On the other hand, in 1798 an English economist named Thomas Malthus argued that "The power of population is indefinitely greater than the power in the earth to produce subsistence for man." In other words, Malthus be-lieved that humankind had a tendency to increase faster than the food supply. Malthus argued that if population growth were not checked by moral restraint (abstaining from having sex and babies), starvation and disease would be the inevitable result.

The argument between the optimism of Frederick and the pessimism of Malthus has become more and more important in recent decades; in the twentieth and twenty-first centuries, the world population has grown as never before. While the human population has been growing for as long as people have kept records, recent generations have seen a rapid acceleration in growth. Experts estimate that the world population was somewhere over 200 million people at the time of the Roman Empire in A.D. 300–400. By 1800, that number had ballooned to more than 975 million people. By 1970 there were more than 3.6 billion people in the world; by 1990 more than 5.2 billion, and by 2009 more than 6.7 billion. In other words, between 1990 and 2009, we have added more people to the world than were alive in 1800. Growth rates are now actually slowing, but demographers think we may add another several billion people, ending with a stable population of about 9 billion by 2050.

The enormous growth of world population in the last hundred years is due to a variety of factors, including agricultural improvements and medical advances that have increased life expectancy. Since no increase like this has ever happened before, it is difficult to say what the effects will be on the global environment or society. No one knows if, or when, we will face a worldwide Malthusian catastrophe, nor exactly what it would look like if we did.

While the world as a whole has never seen this kind of exponential growth, more contained societies have seen relatively large increases in population. By looking at these societies, experts have tried to determine what population growth means for the globe as a whole.

In his 2005 book *Collapse*, geographer and ecologist Jared Diamond looked to Easter Island to try to understand population growth and resource depletion. Easter Island is a nine-mile long island in the southeast Pacific Ocean. More than 1,250 miles from its closest inhabited neighbor, Easter Island is one of the most isolated places on earth. It was probably colonized by Polynesians rowing from other islands sometime before A.D. 900, and after that there is little evidence that it traded or had any contact with its neighbors. Nonetheless,

Diamond argues, the island was home to a large and vibrant culture. By the 1600s, Diamond believes that there were between fifteen thousand and thirty thousand people on the island, or several hundred people per square mile. In addition, this population was able, without cranes or even wheels, to carve and position a series of massive carved stone heads, some weighing up to 12 tons. These enormous statues are so impressive that a few writers have argued they must have been built by aliens (though researchers, and, for that matter, the Easter Islanders themselves, don't take this theory seriously). Dragging the statues into position required vast quantities of timber to create sleds—timber that was also used to build the canoes with which the islanders fished and traveled.

In the 1600s Easter Island was a fairly populous nation with plentiful wood, capable of massive public projects. By the time the first Europeans arrived on the island in the late 1700s, however, Easter Island was home to probably only a few thousand people. Moreover, the island had no trees, and the building of the stone monuments had ceased. The reason, according to Diamond, was a Malthusian disaster. To support their population, the islanders cleared land for agriculture. They cut down even more trees to create the sleds and levers they needed to move the giant stone heads. Eventually, there were no trees left, which meant that the soil eroded, canoes couldn't be built, and the economy collapsed. The result was war, starvation, and even cannibalism.

In the fate of Easter Island's people, Diamond sees an analog for our planet, where a rapidly growing population and an even more rapidly growing consumption of resources may lead to or exacerbate water shortages, food shortages, deforestation, and global warming. "When the Easter Islanders got into difficulty," Diamond says, "there was nowhere to which they could flee, nor to which they could turn for help; nor shall we modern Earthlings have recourse elsewhere if our troubles increase. Those are the reasons why people see the collapse of Easter Island society as a metaphor, a worst-case scenario, for what may lie ahead of us in our own future."

For Diamond, then, as for Malthus, resources are finite, and growth in human population and consumption requires changes in behavior that lead to lower birthrates and moderated consumption if we are to avoid disaster. This view is by and large the most popular among policy experts.

However, the contrary view put forward by Frederick the Great has not gone away. Some experts argue that scientific solutions in the past have prevented Malthusian catastrophe. In his 1968 book *The Population Bomb*, Paul Ehrlich predicted that the 1970s would see massive famine with "hundreds of millions of people" starving to death. Instead, uses of chemical fertilizers and other innovations led to the Green Revolution in agriculture. Already underway when Ehrlich wrote his book, the Green Revolution transformed farming worldwide, so that, for example, Mexico went from importing wheat in 1943 to exporting half a million tons of the grain in 1964. Pointing to innovations like these, economist Julian Simon argued in his book *The Ultimate Resource* that "It is your mind that matters economically, as much or more than your mouth or hands. In the long run, the most important economic effect of population size and growth is the contribution of additional people to our stock of useful knowledge. And this contribution is large enough in the long run to overcome all the costs of population growth."

Global Viewpoints: Population Growth looks at the advantages and disadvantages of population growth in different nations and regions throughout the world. The first chapter looks at the link between population growth and hunger. The second examines the environmental impact of population growth. The third looks at how population growth may impact economic growth, both positively and negatively. And the final chapter explores how social factors like war, democracy, religion, and cultural differences impact changes in population.

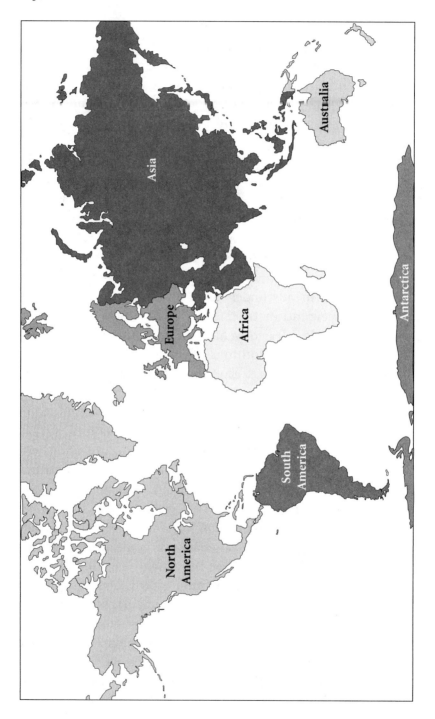

Population Growth and Hunger

The United States Must Support Family Planning to Reduce Poverty and World Hunger

Sneha Barot

Sneha Barot works in the Washington, DC office of the Guttmacher Institute as a senior public policy associate on issues of international family planning and abortion, reproductive health products and technologies, and racial and ethnic disparities in health care. The Guttmacher Institute is an organization that advocates sexual and reproductive health worldwide. In the following viewpoint, Barot argues that the United States needs to increase its funding for international family planning in order to improve maternal health, advance child survival, reduce women's recourse to abortion, and promote economic growth and social stability. Barot points out that "Failure to adopt family planning services has been identified as a key factor in the world's current food crisis."

As you read, consider the following questions:

1. According to Barot, how many women in the world do not have access to the contraceptives they need?

2. According to Barot, how many unintended pregnancies could be avoided through the use of contraceptives?

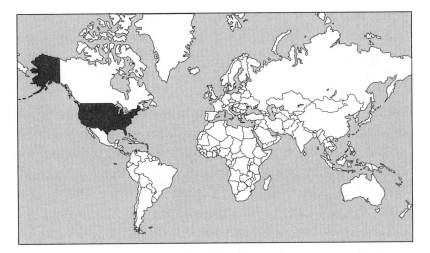

3. According to Barot, how is family planning and economic stability at the household level reflected at the community and national levels?

Contributions from the U.S. government to voluntary family planning activities in developing countries have generated considerable successes over the last four decades. Yet, the U.S. family planning and reproductive health program, administered primarily through the U.S. Agency for International Development (USAID), has encountered and continues to face many roadblocks to further progress, including policy impediments to sound programming imposed by the government itself. Such self-imposed setbacks include the "Mexico City" policy, also known as the global gag rule, which renders local organizations that engage in privately funded abortion-related activities consistent with their own country's laws ineligible for U.S. support for contraceptive services. Additional policy constraints involve withdrawal of U.S. assistance to the United Nations Population Fund (UNFPA) on the grounds that UNFPA's support of voluntary contraceptive services in China is somehow tantamount to support of coercive abortion. While these policy problems have caused serious injury and will require repair, an equally important challenge for

21

policy makers under a new presidential administration will be to remedy the trend of chronic underfunding of international family planning programs.

Needs and Unmet Needs

Over the last 30 years, as women in the developing world increasingly have desired smaller families, contraceptive use has risen and fertility rates have fallen. Still, demographic surveys indicate that the actual family size in most developing countries remains greater than the desired family size. This gap between the real and the ideal persists even in Sub-Saharan Africa, which still retains a preference for larger families and has the highest fertility rates in the world.

According to "Adding It Up," a joint report from the Guttmacher Institute and UNFPA, a total of $7.1 billion (in 2003 dollars) is spent annually on family planning services in the developing world. These funds—from both donor countries and recipient developing countries themselves—support contraceptive care for 504 million women, helping them to avoid 187 million unintended pregnancies and 60 million unplanned births. However, approximately 201 million women in developing countries desire to either delay or limit their births, but do not have access to modern contraceptives; 64 million of these women use traditional methods such as periodic abstinence and withdrawal, which have high failure rates. The report concludes that providing family planning services to all of these women would prevent an additional 52 million unintended pregnancies and a wide range of deleterious outcomes from those pregnancies.

Preventing Adverse Outcomes

Averting an additional 52 million unintended pregnancies annually would prevent:

- 23 million unplanned births
- 22 million abortions

- 7 million miscarriages

- 1.4 million infant deaths

- 142,000 pregnancy-related deaths—53,000 from unsafe abortion and 89,000 from other causes

- 505,000 children from losing their mothers

Unlike the provision of some types of health care, such as childhood immunizations, meeting the need for contraceptive services is an ongoing imperative. The typical woman who wants only two children (increasingly the worldwide norm) will be pregnant, postpartum or seeking pregnancy for only a few years of her life, but she will need to use contraceptives to avoid additional pregnancies for some three decades. And the challenge only escalates as population growth itself increases, currently driven by 1.2 billion adolescents, the largest cohort of adolescents in history, who are approaching reproductive maturity and will need access to sexual and reproductive health information and services in the coming decades.

High-risk pregnancies—those that come too early, too often or too late in life—increase a woman's risk of pregnancy-related death.

A Plethora of Benefits

The United States has long been and remains the single largest donor country for population assistance in the world. Yet, over the last quarter century, its position as global leader has been compromised by politically motivated programmatic restrictions imposed by successive presidential administrations, restrictions that have themselves been echoed in diminished levels of financial support. The bottom line is that at $461 million, current U.S. funding is only a small fraction of what it should be, according to the formulation derived at the 1994 International Conference on Population and Development in Cairo, Egypt.

As a result, international family planning advocates are embarking on an ambitious goal of more than doubling current funding to $1 billion. This amount—itself less than a third of the $3.2 billion it should be, according to updated estimates—is more than justified, because family planning is the key means to a broad range of critically important individual and societal development goals. First and foremost, of course, family planning enables women and couples to control their own reproductive destinies, an essential human freedom. At the same time, by preventing unintended, often high-risk pregnancies, family planning also saves women's lives and protects their health; improves infant survival rates and bolsters child health; reduces women's recourse to abortion and, especially, unsafe abortion; protects women and their partners against sexually transmitted infections (STIs), including HIV/AIDS; enhances women's status and promotes equality between men and women; fosters social and economic development and security at the family, community and country level; and helps safeguard the environment. These are compelling reasons, individually and collectively, to ramp up financial investment in international family planning programs.

Improving Maternal Health

A woman's ability to control the timing, spacing and total number of her children is critical to preserving her life and health. High-risk pregnancies—those that come too early, too often or too late in life—increase a woman's risk of pregnancy-related death. The impact of birth spacing alone on maternal mortality is dramatic. According to the World Bank, maternal mortality would drop by 25-35% if the unmet need for family planning were fulfilled for the estimated 137 million women in the developing world who are neither using a traditional nor a modern contraceptive method.

In addition, better timing and spacing of births could reduce the estimated 15 million women each year who face illness or disability from pregnancy-related complications, which in turn result in negative financial, social and health consequences for the women, their families and their communities. Insufficiently spaced pregnancies, along with inadequate prenatal, delivery and postpartum care, can jeopardize a woman's health on a temporary or permanent basis, through such conditions as anemia, obstetric fistula, hemorrhage, hypertension, infection and infertility.

Advancing Child Survival

Another high-impact public health benefit of family planning is in the area of child health and survival. USAID research shows that infants born closely together are at considerably higher risk of dying before their first birthday than are those with wider birth intervals. In fact, if women in developing countries could space their births three years apart, infant and under-five mortality rates would fall by 24% and 35%, respectively. The benefits of these longer birth intervals would also improve other health and nutrition indicators, such as the risk of stunting and underweight children.

The ability to delay births becomes even more important for the millions of young women who enter marriage at an early age. Adolescents are more vulnerable to complications of pregnancy and maternal death. Similarly, infants born to teen mothers, rather than women in their 20s and 30s, have double the risk of dying during their first year.

Reducing Women's Recourse to Abortion

The undeniable philosophical and political issues associated with abortion, at the individual and country level, are exacerbated in the context of the developing world, where abortions are largely illegal and unsafe. According to a 2007 study conducted by the World Health Organization (WHO) and the

---

Effects of the Global Gag Rule

The Global Gag Rule has cost the Family Guidance Association of Ethiopia (FGAE), the largest reproductive health provider in the country, more than half a million dollars. FGAE operates 18 clinics, 24 youth service centers, 671 community-based reproductive health care sites, and hundreds of other sites for health care provision. Due to lack of funds, services to 229,947 men and 301,054 women in urban areas have been eliminated.

Due to the Global Gag Rule, Marie Stopes International Kenya was forced to close a clinic located in Kisumu, a province where HIV prevalence is the highest in the country. When it closed, services for STI [sexually transmitted infections] screening and treatment, HIV testing and counseling, along with other basic family planning and reproductive health care, ended for a community of 300,000 people.

Kate Francis and Amy Leipziyer,
"The Global Gag Rule: Bleak Choices and Cruel Effects,"
Population Connection, *2004. www.populationconnection.org.*

Guttmacher Institute, more than half (55%) of abortions in developing countries are unsafe; that proportion reaches as high as 95% in Africa and Latin America. Almost all abortion-related deaths occur in developing countries, accounting for 13% of overall maternal deaths worldwide.

Numerous studies have found that women in countries where abortion is illegal resort to abortion at similar rates as those living in countries where the procedure is legal. The most effective and efficient tool to prevent abortions is to prevent unintended pregnancies in the first place through the use of family planning. In the developing world, two-thirds of unintended pregnancies occur among women who are not using any method of contraception. In these countries, almost one-fifth of all pregnancies end in induced abortion. Satisfying the unmet need for contraception in these countries would further reduce women's recourse to abortion, beyond the substantial progress already made by current contraceptive use.

Preventing STIs, Including HIV/AIDS

Women who are sexually active are exposed to the dual risks of unintended pregnancy and STIs. The WHO cites unsafe sex as the second most important risk factor for disease, disability or death in the poorest countries. STIs, including HIV, are one of the leading causes of loss of healthy life among women. Women in their reproductive years are the fastest growing group of people contracting HIV, comprising more than half of those currently living with the virus.

Education delays women's age at marriage and first birth, and contraceptive use decreases the likelihood that young women will drop out of school because of pregnancy.

Use of barrier methods of contraception—namely, the male and female condom—reduces the spread of STIs such as HIV from one partner to another—so-called horizontal transmission. Female condoms are particularly important, as they are the only available woman-controlled method that effectively protects against the sexual transmission of HIV. Additionally, by preventing pregnancies and births, all contraceptives play a significant role in prevention of "vertical transmission" of HIV. Although dedicated prevention of mother-to-child transmission (PMTCT) programs in developing countries substantially reduce the transmission of the virus to newborns through application of a short course of antiretroviral drugs, these interventions are not known, accessible or used by the vast majority of affected women in poor countries. Thus, it is extremely important to also supply contraceptives to women living with HIV who themselves desire to limit their childbearing. USAID has found that providing contraceptives to HIV-positive women who wish to avoid pregnancy could help prevent almost twice the number of child infections and almost four times the number of child deaths than stand-alone PMTCT programs.

Raising Women's Status

Beyond its medical benefits, investment in family planning generates powerful returns in other areas. The ability to control one's fertility is fundamental to raising women's status in society. Women who can decide when and how many children to have will be better positioned to negotiate decision-making in their households and to increase their life choices. Of particular importance is women's increased capacity to take advantage of educational and economic opportunities, and to enhance financial security at the household level. Women who cannot control the timing of their births are often doomed to poverty, as they struggle to raise more children than they would desire.

The impacts of fertility control and the education of young women are interrelated—both are necessary agents in improving women's status and contributing to a country's development. Education delays women's age at marriage and first birth, and contraceptive use decreases the likelihood that young women will drop out of school because of pregnancy. According to an analysis by the Millennium Project, among unmarried, sexually active, 15-17-year-old females, those enrolled in school were more likely than those not in school to use contraceptives. Another report by the POLICY Project estimated that 8-25% of young women in certain Sub-Saharan African countries drop out of school because of unwanted pregnancies. Not only does family planning help women avail themselves of schooling, but educated mothers and smaller families increase the likelihood that children, especially daughters, are also more educated.

Promoting Economic Growth and Social Stability

Family planning is essential to building socially and economically stronger families and fighting poverty. Families that can choose the number, timing and spacing of their children are better able to plan their lives, to save resources and to increase their household income. Families with more children have a higher risk of falling into poverty. Having fewer children allows parents to invest in their existing children and provide adequate nutrition, housing and education for the entire family. Moreover, women who control their fertility have more time for their own development and are more able to socially and politically participate in their communities.

The relationship between family planning and economic stability at the household level is also reflected at the community and national levels. Reduction of high fertility is a necessary although not sufficient factor in a country's path to economic development. According to a 2007 United Kingdom Parliament report on population, lower fertility accounts for 25-40% of economic growth in developing countries. Family planning decreases morbidity and mortality rates, and thereby produces a healthier and more productive workforce. Lower population growth reduces the burden on countries to make public expenditures for orphan care, family subsidies, food aid, health care, education and other social services.

The relationship between fertility and development has implications for a country's security as well. Expanding populations in poor regions can cause competition for limited resources, such as food, housing, schools and jobs, which in turn, can lead to societal instability. Failure to adopt family planning services has been identified as a key factor in the world's current food crisis. In the Philippines, for example, the government's refusal to support family planning services has been linked to a serious state of food insecurity. Explaining this phenomenon in a recent *Washington Post* article, a Filipino economics professor noted: "Even when there is widespread corruption, insurgent violence and other powerful reasons for poverty, the evidence from across Asia is that good population policy by itself contributes to significant poverty reduction."

Protecting the Environment

In the latter half of the 20th century, the earth's population more than doubled to six billion. It is expected to grow to more than nine billion by 2050, with almost all of the net increase occurring in developing countries that are least able and prepared to absorb this expansion. Unfortunately, millions of women in these countries currently wish to have smaller families—which would curb population growth—but do not have access to modern contraceptive methods that would help them achieve their childbearing goals.

There is a complex relationship among the effects of consumption and population growth on global environmental sustainability. One aspect of that relationship is that the rapid depletion of environmental resources in many poor countries is occurring to meet the needs of growing, migrating, urbanizing, and aging populations. These population pressures are straining the world's resources by diminishing safe water supplies, increasing carbon emissions, deforesting lands, and polluting the air and oceans. For example, the United Nations (UN) estimates that by 2025, more than three billion people will live in water-stressed countries, where basic water requirements for cooking, drinking and hygiene will be at risk. Climate change will contribute to less rainfall in regions such as North Africa, while demand for water in these areas will rise.

Lack of adequate and safe water will endanger staple food production, exacerbate malnutrition and spread disease from lack of adequate sanitation.

Stepping Up

At a recent conference of the UN Commission on Population and Development, UN Secretary-General Ban Ki-moon and UNFPA Executive Director Thoraya Ahmed Obaid singled out the downward trend in international funding for family planning as endangering the realization of the Millennium Development Goals, established in 2000 to set objectives for addressing poverty, health and women's empowerment in developing countries. A UN report released at the meeting noted that global funding for family planning services plummeted between 1995 and 2006. The Secretary-General warned that this pattern of shrinking funding for family planning poses "serious implications for the ability of countries to address the unmet need for such services, and could undermine efforts to prevent unintended pregnancies and reduce maternal and infant mortality."

Against this backdrop, the United States has a financial and moral obligation to reduce the deficiencies in services, in funding, in policy formulation and in direction for global family planning efforts. Reasserting this leadership begins with overturning the global gag rule and releasing UNFPA funds. It continues with reprioritizing and reinvigorating financial assistance for international family planning activities—assistance that must be sustained over the long haul, since using family planning services is not a one-time event for individuals and couples, but a need that lasts throughout an individual's reproductive life, and will rise globally with increased population growth. Finally, U.S. leadership should serve as a call to action for all countries to step up and put family planning back on the agenda as an important foreign assistance and development issue. Millions of women and families in the developing world are depending on this leadership.

The Philippines Must Slow Population Growth to Combat Food Crisis

Antonio C. Abaya

Antonio C. Abaya is a Filipino columnist, radio commentator, and author. In the following viewpoint, he writes that a rice crisis in the Philippines has pushed the government to acknowledge the necessity of family planning initiatives. The Philippines is a predominantly Roman Catholic country, and so has been reluctant to encourage birth control measures, as the government of Thailand has done. As a result, Abaya asserts, poverty and hunger in the Philippines have been exacerbated. Abaya also says that the government has added to the food crisis by using farmlands to raise biofuel crops rather than food crops.

As you read, consider the following questions:

1. According to Abaya, why is it particularly shameful that the Philippines was the biggest importer of rice in the world in 2007?
2. What were the population growth rates of Thailand and the Philippines in 2007?
3. What global warming gas is produced by the burning of biofuels?

Antonio C. Abaya, "Let Them Eat Bio-fuels," *Manila Standard Today*, April 10, 2008. Reproduced by permission.

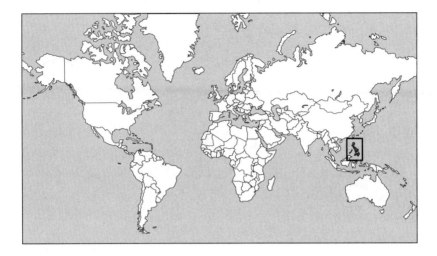

[**P**hilippine] President [Gloria] Arroyo seems to be pushing the panic button—which is good, if you ask me—regarding the developing rice crisis. Perhaps she is heeding the warning that hungry voters mean a sure defeat for the incumbents in the next elections. Does this mean that she will be running for re-election in 2010?

In quick succession this week [April 2008] the National Food Authority [NFA] started selling rice in 1-kilogram bags, instead of by the 50-kg sack, supposedly to discourage the repacking of the cereal by unscrupulous rice dealers who repack the low priced NFA rice and re-sell them as high-priced premium or imported rice.

Upon arrival from Hong Kong, President Arroyo convened the Cabinet right at the Ninoy Aquino International Airport during which she announced that she was authorizing the use of P5 billion [5 billion Philippine pesos] to subsidize the country's rice farmers and ensure a steady supply of the cereal. She also said that local government units could tap the P32-billion budgetary surplus to encourage rice production. . . .

In Thailand, Mechai Means "Condom"

Birth control was not a topic for polite discussion in the 1970s [in Thailand] and access to birth control was restricted to a doctor's prescription. Mechai [Viravaidya, founder and chairman of Population and Community Development Association] challenged that "inside the box" approach and pressed for changes so that nurses, midwives, shopkeepers and hairdressers could distribute birth control pills. "We should have monkeys prescribing!" Mechai erupts during [a] discussion.

Population and Community Development stepped even further out of Thailand's public health policy box with a public education blitz to de-stigmatize public discussion of sex and contraception in Thai society. Mechai invited Buddhist monks to bless contraceptives with holy water. Mechai and his Population and Community Development team wrote family planning jingles, dreamed up a vasectomy tour bus, awarded non-pregnancy agricultural credits and promoted condom-blowing competitions among students and teachers in Thai schools. These were gimmicks but they succeeded in helping to reduce family size. By 2000, Thailand's population had dropped to 1.6 children per family and an annual population growth rate of 0.8 percent.

Erica Trutus Burman,
"Condom King," Worldview Magazine,
Fall 2006.

More People, Less Food

Easily the most positive side effect of the rice crisis is the realization, *finally*, by Congress (and hopefully by President Arroyo as well) that the food crisis is exacerbated by the population crisis, that this country will never be self-sufficient in food as long as the population continues to gallop away to a Standing-Room-Only scenario.

According to *Standard Today*, the budget for family planning is being increased this year [2008] from P200 million to P2 billion, of which P800 million will be used for an education-information campaign to help couples decide which method of birth control they will adopt; and P1.2 billion will be used for condoms and birth control pills that are "medically and legally permissible," for free distribution to poor families, according to Rep. Edcel Lagman of Albay.

This country will never be self-sufficient in food as long as the population continues to gallop away to a Standing-Room-Only scenario.

This country has not been self-sufficient in rice since the mid-1960s, after which we have had to import the cereal, year after year after year. In 2007, we became the biggest rice importer in the world, which is a shameful distinction since we are host to the International Rice Research Institute in Los Baños, where agriculturists from all over South and Southeast Asia have learned the most modern technologies for growing rice.

Our problem is population. We are having more children faster than we can grow the food to feed them. The most graphic illustration of this is a comparison of the Philippines with Thailand. . . .

In the 1970s, the Philippines and Thailand had about the same population size, about 45 million. But because Thailand had an active and comprehensive population management program, and the Philippines did not, in 2007 there were 89 million Filipinos, but only 65 million Thais.

Better Planning in Thailand

That surplus of 24 million more mouths to feed encapsulates the failure of this country. By all yardsticks of common sense, it is easier to feed, house, clothe, educate and find jobs for 65 million people than for 89 million. And yet, except during the presidency of the Protestant Fidel Ramos, succeeding governments failed or refused to appreciate that truism, largely because the politicians were terrified of incurring the wrath of the Roman Catholic bishops.

Hopefully, not anymore, if that P1.2-billion budget for condoms pushes through this year [2008]. In Thailand, the lynchpin of their population management program was the free distribution of condoms. The bureaucrat who implemented that program was so successful in it that his surname, Mechai, became the Thai word for condom.

Because Thailand had an active and comprehensive population management program, and the Philippines did not, in 2007 there were 89 million Filipinos, but only 65 million Thais.

Compare the population growth rates of Thailand and the Philippines, and weep: In 1985, it was 1.7 percent for Thailand, and 2.4 percent for the Philippines. It was 1.3 and 2.8 percent in 1990; it was 1.2 and 2.3 in 1995; it was 0.9 and 2.17 in 2000; it was 0.68 and 1.95 in 2006; and 0.66 and 1.91 in 2007.

The other country, besides Thailand, that the Philippines buys its rice from, Vietnam, had a population growth rate of 2.5 percent in 1985, 2.5 in 1990, 1.9 in 1995, 1.53 in 2000, and 1.04 in 2007. Which also indicates a deliberate and successful program of population management. Both Thailand and Vietnam are predominantly Buddhist and have no religious hang-ups about the use of artificial methods of birth control.

Stuck in a Bio-fuels Sinkhole

As if being predominantly Roman Catholic were not handicap enough, we have the additional burden of having been suckered into the bio-fuel [fuels derived from crops] stampede. President Arroyo and Senator Juan Miguel Zubiri, no doubt with the noblest intentions, convinced us to follow the global rush of converting farmlands into plantations for bio-fuel crops. Rep. Roilo Golez seems to have been the only person in Congress to take a contrarian view.

I wrote in my article titled "Wayang in Bali" of Dec. 17, 2007 that bio-fuels were not a wise alternative to fossil fuels. I wrote that burning bio-fuels would still result in the emission of carbon dioxide, the perceived culprit in global warming. Furthermore, converting millions of hectares of farmlands from food crops to bio-fuel crops—sugarcane, rapeseeds, jatropha trees, etc.—has reduced food harvests worldwide and has consequently raised the prices of food staples. When I wrote that article, the price of our pan de sal [a rounded bread usually eaten at breakfast] had just increased from P2 to P2.50 per piece, due to the higher cost of wheat.

Now we and the rest of the world are stuck in a giant bio-fuels sinkhole that has raised food prices worldwide so high that the specter of food rations and food riots have been raised. For the same reason, our government is pressing the panic button as fears of a rice shortage become self-fulfilling.

As if being predominantly Roman Catholic were not handicap enough, we have the additional burden of having been suckered into the bio-fuel stampede.

In a brutally frank cover story in its April 7 issue, *Time* magazine calls it "The Clean Energy Scam," with the following blurb: "Hyped as an eco-friendly fuel, ethanol increases global warming, destroys forests and inflates food prices." Warns *Time*: "The bio-fuels boom . . . is one that could haunt the planet for generations—and it is only getting started. . . ."

Not enough food on the table? Let them eat bio-fuels.

Asia and Africa Face a Dangerous Reduction in Farmland as Population Grows

Janet Larsen

Janet Larsen is the director of research at the Earth Policy Institute. In the following viewpoint, she argues that in the past, food supplies have grown because of an increase in land under cultivation. Larsen explains that most good agricultural land is already under cultivation, and that there is unlikely to be any further expansion of agricultural land. As population grows and cropland remains the same, Larsen says, the ratio of cropland area per person will shrink. Larsen concludes that if population growth is not slowed, countries such as Pakistan and Nigeria will not be able to produce enough grain to feed their people.

As you read, consider the following questions:

1. What six countries account for half of the world's annual population growth?
2. According to Larsen, Nigeria's grainland doubled since 1950, while what happened to its population?
3. According to Larsen, if world grainland area stays the same, how many hectares of grainland will there be per person in 2050?

Janet Larsen, "Population Growth Leading to Land Hunger," Earth Policy Institute, January 23, 2003. Reproduced by permission.

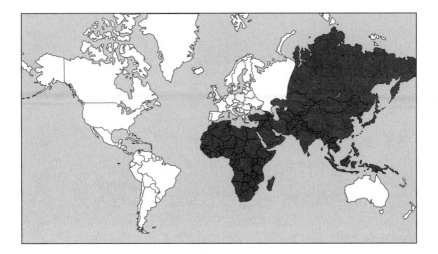

From the beginning of agriculture until the middle of the twentieth century, increases in world food production have come largely from expanding agricultural land. Between 1950 and 1981, the area in grain expanded from 587 million hectares to its historical peak of 732 million hectares (1 hectare = 2.47 acres). By 2000 it had fallen to 656 million hectares. Meanwhile, with population expanding from 2.5 billion in 1950 to 6.1 billion in 2000, the cropland area per person shrank from 0.23 to 0.11 hectares—an area half the size of a housing lot in suburban America.

The world's grain area is unlikely to expand much, if at all, during the next half-century. Low grain prices in recent years have led some farmers to pull back from the more marginal lands, while others have abandoned degraded fields. In addition, agriculture has lost millions of hectares of farmland that have been paved over or covered by urban sprawl.

Where there is limited arable land, fast-growing populations can shrink cropland area per person to the point where countries can no longer feed themselves. Governments that can afford it then compensate by importing grain—the source of more than half the calories humans consume directly. But in countries that cannot import grain, people go hungry.

Where Cropland Is Scarce

Cropland scarcity has forced some densely populated Asian countries to import most of their grain. After several decades of shrinking per capita grainland, farmers in Malaysia now cultivate only 0.03 hectares of grain for each resident. Japan, South Korea, and Taiwan each harvest less than 0.02 hectares. To make up for production shortfalls, these four countries currently import more than 70 percent of the grain they consume, leaving them vulnerable to supply disruptions.

Egypt is following close behind. It harvests 0.04 hectares of grainland for each of its 70 million people and imports over 40 percent of its grain. With the water from the Nile River now fully used, and with Egypt's population increasing by over 1 million annually, this share of imports will almost certainly climb.

Fast-growing populations can shrink cropland area per person to the point where countries can no longer feed themselves. . . . In countries that cannot import grain, people go hungry.

Half of the world's annual population growth of 77 million people occurs in just six countries—India, China, Pakistan, Nigeria, Bangladesh, and Indonesia. Each of these nations faces a steady shrinkage of grainland per person and thus risks heavy future dependence on grain imports. This raises two important questions. Will these countries be able to afford to import large quantities of grain as land hunger increases? And will grain markets be able to meet their additional demands?

India, Pakistan, and China

In India, where one out of every four people is undernourished, 16 million people are added to the population each year. The grain area per person in India has shrunk steadily for several decades and is now below 0.10 hectares—less than half that in 1950. As land holdings are divided for inheritance with each succeeding generation, the 48 million farms that averaged 2.7 hectares each in 1960 were split into 105 million farms half that size in 1990, when India's grainland expansion peaked. The average Indian family, which now has three children, will be hard pressed to pass on viable parcels of land to future generations.

Pakistan, with five children per family, is growing even more rapidly. In 1988, Pakistan's National Commission on Agriculture was already linking farm fragmentation and a rising reliance on marginal lands to declining farm productivity in some areas. Since then, the country has grown from just over 100 million to almost 150 million. Its per person grain area is now less than 0.09 hectares.

In India, where one out of every four people is under-nourished . . . the grain area per person . . . has shrunk steadily for several decades and is now below 0.10 hectares—less than half that in 1950.

In China, the grain area per person has also shrunk dramatically to a diminutive 0.07 hectares, down from 0.17 hectares in 1950. Shifting agricultural production to higher-value crops, like fruits and vegetables, and converting farms to forest for conservation accounts for some of the grainland contraction, along with losses to nonfarm uses such as buildings and roads.

Though the shrinkage of farmland available per person in China has slowed in concert with declining family size, this country—whose population of 1.3 billion is as large as the entire world's in 1850—is still expected to add 187 million people to its ranks in the next 50 years. The robustness of

Grain Area Per Person

Country	1950	Grainland Per Person Hectares 2000	2050 (projected)
Australia	0.73	0.97	0.70
Canada	1.42	0.59	0.45
United States	0.51	0.21	0.15
Nigeria	0.26	0.15	0.06
Ethiopia	0.26	0.11	0.04
Mexico	0.19	0.10	0.07
India	0.22	0.10	0.06
Tanzania	0.07	0.09	0.04
Pakistan	0.18	0.09	0.04
Bangladesh	0.20	0.09	0.04
Indonesia	0.10	0.07	0.05
China	0.17	0.07	0.06
Uganda	0.15	0.06	0.01
North Korea	0.14	0.05	0.04
Egypt	0.08	0.04	0.02
Democratic Republic of Congo (Zaire)	0.05	0.04	0.01
Malaysia	0.09	0.03	0.02
Rwanda	0.06	0.03	0.01
South Korea	0.10	0.03	0.02
Japan	0.06	0.02	0.02
World	0.23	0.11	0.07

Conversion: 1 hectare = 2.47 acres

TAKEN FROM: Janet Larsen, "Population Growth Leading to Land Hunger," Earth Policy Institute, 2003. http://www.earth-policy.org.

China's economy enables it to turn to world markets to import grain, but this does not guarantee that those markets can support massive additional demand without hefty price increases.

Cropland in Africa

The scarcity of arable cropland in sub-Saharan Africa helps to explain the region's declining production per person in recent decades. Nigeria, for example, Africa's most populous country, has seen its population quadruple since 1950 while its grainland area doubled—effectively halving the grainland per person. In northern Nigeria, pastoralists and farmers fleeing the encroaching Sahara, which annually claims 350,000 hectares of land (about half the size of the U.S. state of Delaware), have increased demands on the already scarce land elsewhere in the country, sparking ethnic tensions.

With most of the planet's arable land already under the plow and with additional cropland being paved over and built on each year, there is little chance that the world grain area will rebound

.

The experience in Rwanda, Africa's most densely populated country, highlights the potentially serious ramifications of land scarcity. Between 1950 and 1990, Rwanda's population tripled from 2.1 million to 6.8 million. The per capita grainland availability fell to 0.03 hectares. James Gasana, Rwanda's Minister of Agriculture and Environment in 1990–92, has noted that rapid population growth led to farm fragmentation, land degradation, deforestation, and famine. These stresses ignited the undercurrent of ethnic strife, erupting in civil war in the early 1990s and culminating in horrific genocide in 1994, when some 800,000 people were killed. Gasana points out that violence was concentrated in the communes where the food supply was inadequate.

A 2000 headline from the Pan African News Agency, discussing a ministry of lands survey, read "Rwanda: Land Scarcity May Jeopardize Peace Process." Now with a population that has rebounded to 8.1 million, and with the average family having six children, pressure on the land in Rwanda is again mounting.

Grainland's Shrinking Future

Most of the 3 billion people to be added to the world population in the next 50 years will be born in areas where land resources are scarce. If world grainland area stays the same as in 2000, the 9 billion people projected to inhabit the planet in 2050 would each be fed from less than 0.07 hectares of grainland—an area smaller than what is available per person today in land-hungry countries like Bangladesh, Pakistan, and Afghanistan.

By 2050, India and Nigeria would cultivate 0.06 hectares of grainland for each person, less than one tenth the size of a soccer field. China, Pakistan, Bangladesh, and Ethiopia would drop even lower, to 0.04–0.05 hectares of grainland per person. Faring worse would be Egypt and Afghanistan with 0.02 hectares, as well as Yemen, the Democratic Republic of the Congo, and Uganda, with just 0.01 hectares. These numbers are in stark contrast to those of the less densely populated grain exporters, which may have upwards of 10 times as much grainland per person. For Americans, who live in a country with 0.21 hectares of highly productive grainland per person, surviving from such a small food production base is difficult to comprehend.

With most of the planet's arable land already under the plow and with additional cropland being paved over and built on each year, there is little chance that the world grain area will rebound. At the same time, the annual rise in cropland productivity of 2 percent from 1950 to 1990 has decreased to scarcely 1 percent since 1990, and may drop further in the years ahead. This slowing of productivity gains at a time when the land available per person is still shrinking underlines the urgency of slowing world population growth.

Ethiopia Must Reverse the Cycle of Population Growth, Deforestation, and Starvation

Mestawet Taye Asfaw

Mestawet Taye Asfaw is a food science specialist from Ethiopia and the recipient of the 2007 UNESCO-L'ORÉAL International Fellowship for Women in Science. In the following selection, she talks about how population growth in Ethiopia led people to clear more and more forestland for farms. Asfaw explains that destroying forests results in ecological imbalance: erosion, poor soil quality, and drought. The drought has resulted in widespread famine. To correct these problems, Asfaw says, the government needs to actively pursue sustainable policies, such as ending deforestation and promoting family planning to reduce population growth.

As you read, consider the following questions:

1. According to Asfaw, what caused hunger to become a serious problem in Ethiopia?
2. How do trees improve the quality of air that humans and animals breathe?
3. Does Ethiopia have many rivers?

Mestawet Taye Asfaw, "Ethiopia: What Went Wrong?" agora.forwomeninscience.com, September 28, 2007. Reproduced by permission.

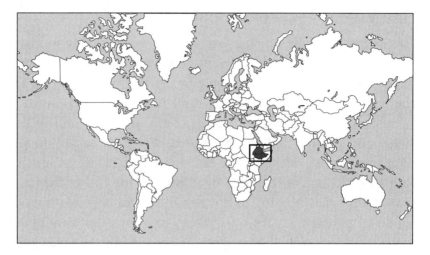

Ethiopia has become a symbol for hunger throughout the world. As an Ethiopian studying abroad I am more aware of this than ever. Please let me begin by telling what happened to me here in Norway where I am currently living. I was waiting in line at a bank. A very old man with a cane was also waiting, and he asked me where I was from. I told him I was from Ethiopia. He said something to the people around us in Norwegian, and suddenly everyone was looking at me with amazement. I did not understand what was being said and why I had become the center of attention. He turned to me again and said. "But, you do not have food in Ethiopia right?" I felt something burning inside me. I started by saying. "No, it's not like that," but I could not continue and suddenly my eyes filled with tears.

The man's question had set me thinking about what I had seen in a drought-stricken village. Babies waiting to die, literally nothing but skin on bones, with no flesh in between. Mothers looking at their babies hopelessly, knowing they could not do anything for them. Once again as I write this, my eyes fill with tears.

The Vicious Cycle of Drought

My father was killed in the war when I was four. My mother and I went to stay with distant relatives until the war was over. There were so many people in the house that needed to be fed that they could not give all of us food regularly. I would say to my mother, "Mama, I am hungry." She would weep and answer that she did not have money to buy food. But this is not real hunger. I did not eat breakfast or lunch, but I usually had at least one small meal at the end of the day. Real hunger has nothing to do with the uncomfortable feeling of an empty stomach for a few hours or even a day. Real hunger is no food in the house, nothing growing in the fields and no money to buy anything. Real hunger is people dying and livestock dying because drought has left them with nothing, absolutely nothing to eat anywhere.

When a drought begins farmers stop selling their animals. They wait for rain to come because they want to be able to feed their animals so they can fatten them up before taking them to market. But rain never comes, feed crops die and the animals begin to waste away. It's already too late, but they take the animals to market, and they are offered next to nothing for them. They herd the animals back home thinking they couldn't afford to sell at such low prices. But the next time they go to market, there are no buyers at all. They return home once again, and the animals die because now there is absolutely nothing left for them to eat.

Babies waiting to die, literally nothing but skin on bones, with no flesh in between. Mothers looking at their babies hopelessly, knowing they could not do anything for them.

Drought and Hunger

Hunger was not a serious problem in Ethiopia country 60 or 70 years ago. What happened? What went wrong? Drought.

Drought is defined as an extended period of months or years when there is a deficiency in water supply. This can range from a period of no rain at all to a period of lower than average rainfall.

I would now like to summarize what I think are causes for drought, and what we should do, but this is only my view and others may have different ideas.

In developing countries the population is continually growing. The economies of most developing countries are based on agriculture. In Ethiopia, about 85% of the population lives from farming. Since the population is always increasing, more food must be grown and therefore more forest land must be cleared for cultivation. A corollary to such continuous population growth, and a further reason for clearing more forest land is that fathers must distribute their property among their children. Over generations the property is divided among more and more individual family members and the acreage becomes insufficient for earning their livelihoods. More untouched forest land is turned to farmland.

Forests have significant implications for human life. Trees improve the quality of the air that humans and animals breathe by trapping carbon [dioxide] and other particles produced by pollution. Trees determine rainfall and replenish the atmosphere. When water is returned to the atmosphere, clouds form and provide another way to block the sun's heat. In short, forests play a key role in regulating climate. As well, trees are important in controlling erosion, preventing landslides, and making the most infertile soil rich with life. Forests are home to a wide variety of species and contribute to conserving biodiversity. Humans are destroying forests and, consequently, their benefits to ourselves and to the environment.

Government Failures

Such deforestation is partly a result of government inaction. Rather than looking for other solutions to hunger and poverty—and here it must be said that they don't always have the

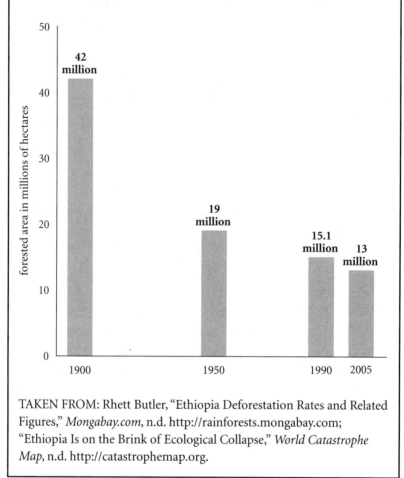

Forestland in Ethiopia, 1900–2005

Ethiopia's forestland has been drastically reduced over the last hundred years. In 1900, 35% of the country was covered in forests. By 2005, that number was reduced to less than 4%.

TAKEN FROM: Rhett Butler, "Ethiopia Deforestation Rates and Related Figures," *Mongabay.com*, n.d. http://rainforests.mongabay.com; "Ethiopia Is on the Brink of Ecological Collapse," *World Catastrophe Map*, n.d. http://catastrophemap.org.

money to provide other solutions—they take the easiest, cheapest and most destructively short-term way out: They simply allow poor farmers to clear forest land. As well, the few remaining high-latitude forests are also threatened by pressure from investors who are converting land for other uses, such as coffee and tea plantations.

When farmers arrive in forested areas they begin by slashing and burning to prepare the land for cultivation. In the short term, the resulting ash acts as fertilizer and the crop yield is good. But the land quickly becomes infertile. The farmer abandons the land with no vegetation cover to prevent erosion. In a short time the resulting erosion causes the land to become useless. I have witnessed this phenomenon with my own eyes in different areas of my country. In Ethiopia, deforestation in only four regions, and the subsequent erosion, is causing the loss of about 1.9 billion tons of soil every year. But a perhaps even more bitter consequence is climate change. When forests disappear it simply means no rain, then drought, then hunger. Some 60 or 70 years ago when 45% of Ethiopia's land area was covered by forests we had no rainfall shortage. Now our vegetation cover is only about 3%. The resulting drop in rainfall means drought again and again, over and over.

A perhaps even more bitter consequence [of deforestation] is climate change. When forests disappear it simply means no rain, then drought, then hunger.

It is important to note—and most people will be surprised to learn this—that Ethiopia has many rivers that flow all year round. Unfortunately, these rivers are usually found in areas that, because of topography, are inaccessible for farming or for harvesting water for irrigation. Along with the food aid for which we are indeed grateful, donor countries could help us with the resources, finances and technologies necessary for bringing this water to dry areas.

Government failure to subsidize agricultural production is, in some cases, the reason for continued deforestation. In Ethiopia the government used to subsidize agriculture, and farmers were able to buy fertilizer for a cheaper price. Fertilizer is now so expensive that farmers who cannot afford to buy it will get very poor yield from their fields and move on to cultivate forest lands.

What Can Be Done

In conclusion, the following is a list of some of the measures we must take to prevent drought and feed our population.

- *Stopping deforestation* Re-vegetation and re-forestation with thorough follow-up after planting. This is not an immediate solution, but it will create a better environment for our children and grandchildren.

- *Drought-tolerant plants* Obviously, plants cannot grow without water, but the scientific community must continue to strive to develop varieties that can do well with little moisture.

- *Developing viable water harvesting technologies/systems*

- *Viable land use policy and corresponding laws*

- *Strategic aid as well as food aid from donor countries* Along with sending food for the needy, donor countries could also try to develop strategies that really take people out of hunger and poverty for the long term. Please let me say that I greatly appreciate the efforts of the many organizations that are trying to help, but the situation might improve more sustainably if they could also help with money or facilities, for example, that would allow us to harvest water from our rivers that are currently inaccessible because of topography and bring that water to our dry regions.

- *Controlling population growth* I think this is an area where Ethiopia is making progress.

- *Encouraging society to develop a sense of collective ownership of the country's resources* Encouraging respect for laws that forbid farmers from grazing their animals on certain national park lands is one example.

The Global Food Crisis Is Not Caused by Overpopulation

Paul Tuns

Paul Tuns is the editor of The Interim, *a Canadian pro-life, pro-family newspaper. In the following viewpoint, Tuns argues that rising food prices are not caused by overpopulation. Instead, he avers, they are the result of a series of one-time catastrophes (like droughts) and non-population related trends (like the growth of affluence in China). Doomsayers such as the early nineteenth century economist Thomas Malthus have often claimed that population would outrun food supply, resulting in disaster. However, Tuns asserts, economic growth and technological innovation have always kept ahead of population growth. Therefore, he claims, politicians should focus on combating malnutrition, not on reducing population. Tuns believes that fears of overpopulation must be reduced in order to combat what he feels are anti-life policies, such as abortion, forced sterilization, and the promotion of contraception.*

As you read, consider the following questions:

1. What did Thomas Malthus think were the "natural checks" that would come into play when population outran food supplies?

2. Has the percentage of people employed as agricultural workers in the United Kingdom increased or decreased since the nineteenth century?

Paul Tuns, "Why Concern with Overpopulation Is Wrong," *Interim*, July 2008. Reproduced by permission.

3. How many children die from malnutrition each year, according to Tuns?

A trip to the grocery store confirms what one reads in the daily paper: food prices are rising dramatically. While Canadian consumers were insulated from the price increases for some time due to the strong dollar and our own agricultural production, in a globalized market, such protections will not last forever. Bread has jumped anywhere between a dime and a quarter per loaf, the cost of milk has increased nearly 5 percent and bags of rice have jumped 10–20 percent.

Yet, food inflation in Canada is lower than elsewhere. According to Statistics Canada, consumer prices for food rose 1.2 percent from April 2007 to April 2008. Grocery bills in Europe rose 7.1 percent over the same period and 5.9 percent in the United States. In the developing world, increases have been even steeper—40 percent in Afghanistan and 22 percent in China. Rising food prices have been devastating to the developing world's poor, who typically spend a quarter to half their income on subsistence food (whereas Canadians typically spend less than 10 percent of household income on food).

In recent months, newspapers and television newscasts have reported on the steeply increasing cost of food and the turmoil it is causing. The World Bank's food price index rose 150 percent from 2002 to January 2008, with half that increase coming since mid-2007.

As a result, countries all over the globe have witnessed food riots and many governments have implemented emergency measures to ration supplies or subsidize food for the poor. Riots over food prices in Bangladesh led the government to postpone elections. The World Food Program has urged members to increase donations; the organization cannot even meet its obligations to provide food relief to the world's poor—the cost of which has increased $700 million in the past year alone—let alone meet new demands that have resulted from the increased cost of food.

Why Are Food Prices Rising?

The reasons for increased food prices across the globe are multiple and varied. Part of the reason is that population is growing, but that does not nearly explain the phenomenon, as population has been growing for centuries, yet both supply and prices go up and down.

The more immediate explanations include the growing middle classes of China, India and other developing world countries which, as they grow richer, want more proteins in their diet; China, for example, is replacing its rice and pork diet with more beef. Cattle require more wheat per pound than do human beings and thus to feed the Chinese beef means livestock farmers require grains that would otherwise be available for human consumption.

Countries all over the globe have witnessed food riots and many governments have implemented emergency measures to ration supplies or subsidize food for the poor.

Also, an unusual number of countries have experienced disturbances to their supply of crops with droughts and floods limiting yields in Canada, the United States and Australia, and hail storms destroying a large number of India's crops. India, normally self-sufficient in rice and grains, has been forced to buy on global markets, increasing upward pressure on food prices.

Another reason is the growing demand for biofuels. The United States is subsidizing ethanol productions, diverting corn from food to fuel; furthermore, many farmers are now growing corn rather than other crops to cash in on the federal subsidies. All this reduces supply and therefore, prices rise as demand grows.

To cope with rising prices, families in the developing world are reducing the number and variety of meals, risking malnutrition. Many commentators have dubbed steeply rising food prices "the silent tsunami," because the devastation it causes does not win the headlines or charitable giving in the way that dramatic natural disasters such as the 2004 South Asia tsunami do.

While food price increases may not stir the popular imagination, they do cause official fretting at international organizations, such as the World Food Program, the Food and Agricultural Organization, the World Bank and the foreign aid establishments in the Western world. While there is genuine hardship associated with these price increases and efforts should be made to alleviate the suffering associated with them, there is little reason for the sort of long-term pessimism that has erroneously informed the neo-Malthusianism behind radical population control measures.

To take but one current example, on its Web site, the Club of Rome names at the top of its list for reasons for food price increases, "the demands of a growing population in many developing countries." But as noted above, there are a myriad of reasons for food price increases; to blame population growth is to fall into a well-worn intellectual trap.

Thomas Malthus and the Fear of Population

Thomas Malthus (1766–1834) first wrote *An Essay on the Principle of Population* in 1798 and updated it five times between then and 1826. He famously predicted that population grew geometrically [for example, 2, 4, 16, 32, and so on] while food supplies grew arithmetically [for example 2, 4, 6, 8, and so on]. "Population, when unchecked, increases in a geometric ratio. Subsistence increases only in an arithmetical ratio." He said if population outstripped the ability of the food supply to feed it, there were natural checks on population growth—

families would have fewer children if they could not feed them or either epidemics or starvation would prune the population. In worst-case scenarios, countries would go to war for resources. In other words, a population's ability to feed itself is generally a check on its own growth.

On the one hand, Malthus, an Anglican country parson, had an agenda. He disliked private and government charity and thus, his observations on population growth justified letting the poor on the streets of London starve to discourage them from having more children.

He also wrote his famous gloomy essay on population, in part, as a reaction against the utopian views of his contemporaries, William Goodwin and the Marquis de Condorcet. Both Goodwin and de Condorcet thought that human beings were perfectible under the right social conditions, a notion with which Malthus (rightly) disagreed. While Goodwin and de Condorcet were too optimistic, Malthus was too pessimistic.

For most of history, 'the only economic growth has been population growth.'

Economic Growth and Population Growth

But on the other hand, Malthus was not entirely wrong, considering the age in which he lived. Up until the beginning of the 19th century, population growth and economic growth, including agricultural production, roughly mirrored each other. His "mistake" as a demographer and economist was living at the precise moment he did. He observed the United States had doubled its population in 25 years and worried that the rest of the world would follow suit.

Tim Harford, a columnist with the *Financial Times* and author of *The Logic of Life: The Rational Economics of an Irrational World*, says for most of history, "the only economic growth has been population growth." The relationship, up to the time of Malthus, worked both ways. To a point, it was reasonable for Malthus to assume his gloomy thesis would be realized.

Angus Maddison, a professor emeritus of economic growth and development at the University of Groningen in the Netherlands, has studied and written about the history of economic growth. In *Contours of the World Economy, 1–2030 AD: Essays in Macro-Economic History*, Maddison noted how population growth follows the same trend as economic growth. He found that in the first millennium after Christ, the world's population increased by less than one-tenth of one percent and the global economy grew about one-sixth of that. Over the next 500 years, population grew 0.1 percent and the economy grew 0.15 percent. Likewise, between 1500 and 1820, the population grew 0.27 percent while the global economy grew 0.32 percent.

The Industrial Revolution was just underway when Malthus began writing his *Essay on Population*, so he would not have noticed that the economy was finally going to grow much faster than the population was.

The Industrial Revolution Changes Everything

From 1820–1870, the economy grew at twice the rate the population did (0.94 percent compared to 0.4 percent), mostly fueled by the use of new technologies (coal-powered factories and steam engines) in Europe.

Over the next four decades, the spread got even larger (2.12 percent economic growth versus 0.80 percent increase in the population). The trend continues through to the present day.

As Tim Harford notes in *The Logic of Life*, "Economists are typically wrong about the future, but few have ever been as spectacularly, famously, and lucklessly wrong as Thomas Malthus."

Malthus was wrong because he did not foresee how the technological improvements of the 19th century would revolutionize agriculture and allow ever-fewer farmers to feed an ever-growing population, nor the benefits of trade. (Nor could he envision refrigerated cargo containers carrying food around the globe.) In Malthus's time, roughly one in three people in the United Kingdom were working in the agricultural, fishing and forestry industries—most of them farmers. Within a century, that number was halved and by 2003, just 1.2 percent of Brits were working within those industries. This would have shocked Malthus; for him, agriculture was a labour-intensive enterprise with most people living a subsistence existence and rural farmers selling their surplus to the cities. No wonder he thought population was imperiled by limited resource growth.

[Thomas] Malthus was spectacularly and famously wrong, yet modern doomsayers continue to spout fears similar to his about overpopulation and impending catastrophe.

While some critics of Malthus, such as Allan Chase, author of *The Legacy of Malthus*, published in 1975, take the early demographer to task for ignoring or failing to understand the change that was occurring at his time, it is often common to miss or miscomprehend phenomena that take place during one's lifetime. But what excuse do his followers have?

Malthus's Heirs

As Harford noted, Malthus was spectacularly and famously wrong, yet modern doomsayers continue to spout fears similar to his about overpopulation and impending catastrophe. The most famous is Paul Ehrlich, author of *The Population Bomb*. Even with the benefit of hindsight—knowledge of the Industrial Revolution that would make Malthus's ideas wrong and obsolete—Ehrlich made the same outrageous claim that population growth would exceed the planet's ability to feed its people. In his best-selling 1968 book, he said, "Too many people—that is why we are on the verge of the 'death rate solution.'" That's Malthus's apocalyptic solution of famine and war to naturally slow down population growth.

Whereas Malthus wrote at the beginning of the Industrial Revolution, Ehrlich was writing as the Green Revolution in agriculture was maximizing farm productivity in Europe and drastically improving it in South Asia. In the 1960s and 1970s, improvements in land management techniques, increased fertilizer use and new technologies (including hybrid plants species) all contributed to greater crop yields and lower food prices. While the Green Revolution largely bypassed Africa, it allowed many countries in southeast Asia to become self-sufficient or nearly self-sufficient.

Yet, Ehrlich was unaware, ignored or did not understand the changes in agriculture that were occurring at this time. He was as wrong as Malthus when he declared, "The battle to feed all of humanity is over. In the 1970s and 1980s, hundreds of millions of people will starve to death in spite of any crash programs embarked upon now. At this late date, nothing can prevent a substantial increase in the world death rate." Yet, population grew across the globe and food disasters such as that experienced by Ethiopia in the mid-1980s were the fault of government distribution policies, rather than an inability to feed the growing population.

Ehrlich's myopia was so extreme that he predicted mass starvation in America by 2000.

Also in 1968, the Club of Rome, a think tank-like group of civil servants from around the world, scientists, economists and business people, was formed. The group was assembled by the Italian businessman Aurelio Peccei, and today it includes the likes of Mikhail Gorbachev. In 1972, the Club of Rome echoed Malthus's doomsday predictions when it released a book-length report, *The Limits [to] Growth*, which would eventually be translated into more than 30 languages and sell 12 million copies. *The Limits [to] Growth* claimed, "If the present growth trends in world population, industrialization, pollution, food production and resource depletion continue unchanged, the limits to growth on this planet will be reached sometime within the next 100 years. The most probable result will be a rather sudden and uncontrollable decline in both population and industrial capacity."

It predicted not only reaching agricultural capacity, but also running out of other commodities, including oil and metals, as well as widespread environmental degradation.

The authors said that the limits of growth would be realized within a century, although there was a sense of urgency that indicated that serious problems were just around the corner. Four decades later, the Club of Rome Web site now claims current food prices might finally be ushering in the gloomy future it predicted in its 1972 manifesto.

It seems that every time that there is an increase in food prices or an environmental catastrophe or the planet reaches a new population milestone like six or seven billion, the nattering nabobs of negativism start bleating about Malthus finally being proven correct. It happened in the 1970s with rising food (and oil) prices and again in the 1990s when there was a slight bump in commodity prices. It is happening again today.

A number of pundits, environmentalists and NGOs [nongovernmental organizations] have again raised the spectre of over-population, saying food prices reflect a world population—slated to increase to 7 billion by 2010—that has (finally) outstripped its capacity to feed everyone. This is bunk. As Nobel prize-winning economist Gary Becker has noted, world prices recently increased by 75 percent in less than one year, but world population did not increase 75 percent over that same span. That is, food price increases are not linked to population growth.

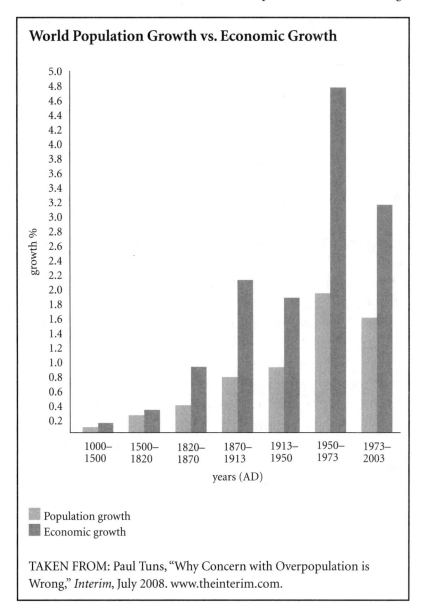

World Population Growth vs. Economic Growth

growth %

years (AD)

Population growth
Economic growth

TAKEN FROM: Paul Tuns, "Why Concern with Overpopulation is Wrong," *Interim*, July 2008. www.theinterim.com.

As noted earlier, there are alternatives and more likely explanations (the developing world is getting richer, inclement weather destroyed an unusual number of crops and the diversion of some agriculture to biofuels). Yet, noted poverty expert Jeffrey Sachs of the Earth Institute at Columbia

University insists that population-control measures are part of any solution to reducing poverty.

World prices recently increased by more than 75 percent in less than one year, but world population did not increase 75 percent over the same span. That is, food price increases are not linked to population growth.

Malthus Is Still Wrong

Considering the evidence that has repeatedly proven Malthus wrong and the fact that there are other, more likely explanations for this food-price crisis, one might reasonably wonder whether some people have an ideological desire to see Malthus's apocalyptic predictions come true. . . .

For the past half-century, there has been what Stephen Mosher of the Population Research Institute dubs the "Population Firm," a group dedicated to using Malthus's population principles as justification to force population control programs upon the developing world.

The "Population Firm" includes academics, NGOs such as Planned Parenthood, supposedly philanthropic foundations and the agencies of the United Nations including UNICEF (which often ties assistance to families to the mother becoming sterilized). . . .

Current food prices will not continue to rise indefinitely, because the market will increase supply. . . . High prices will lead farmers to exploit new, previously unused land for crops and livestock.

Is the current food price crisis different? It is theoretically possible that this is finally the tipping point that Malthus predicted and that Ehrlich said would occur within a century, although his apocalypse was predicted within two decades of publishing his fatuous *The Population Bomb*. The followers of the Russian Communist revolutionary Leon Trotsky used to say the sign of his genius was that 50 years after he made [his predictions] they had not yet become true; he could see so much further into the future than others, they claimed.

Ditto Malthus?

Yet, the perspective of history provides a more sobering analysis of population growth and the prospects for the future, one that embraces humanity rather than sees it as a plague.

The economist Gary Becker has predicted that current food prices will not continue to rise indefinitely, because the market will increase supply. Noting that not all arable land is presently being used for agriculture, high prices will lead farmers to exploit new, previously unused land for crops and livestock. This is especially true in Africa, China and Russia, although it could take up to a decade to get such land producing large-scale crop yields.

Some Solutions

There are also investments in new technologies, including new plant varieties that are able to sustain extreme weather, drought and pests. Genetically modified or hybrid foods might be able to provide nutrients currently unavailable in the diets of those in the developing world. In 2002, during World Youth Day in Toronto, Jim Nicholson, then U.S. ambassador to the Holy See, told the World Youth Alliance that one of his priorities [in] working with Vatican officials was to promote safe, genetically modified foods to combat malnutrition in the developing world. He noted many Africans subsist on a diet of potato and in Asia, on rice; adding vitamins to these staples at the cost of pennies per serving will reduce malnutrition.

But those are long-term solutions.

There are three other reasons to think food prices will decline and food supply will increase.

The first is that [2007] problems were partly caused by more than the normal number of disruptions in the food supply. Droughts in Australia and Africa, floods in China and North America and hailstorms in India all seriously reduced the grain and corn yield.

This provides a perfect storm for food shortages, which drive up grain and rice prices. Record yields are expected in Canada and India this year and production in the United States is expected to return to normal, as the weather seems to have co-operated with increased seeding earlier this year in response to rising food prices.

Another reason for the correction in prices is that high prices are an incentive for developing world producers to improve their productivity. The Green Revolution—improved agricultural practices including fertilization and plant-breeding—missed Africa and there is hope by both political officials and academics there that improved farming techniques will finally take root on that continent.

A relatively modest investment of $300 million would allow micro-nutrients . . . to be added to flour and other staples. That would eliminate childhood deaths from malnutrition.

Another problem is the diversion of some agri-products from food stuffs to fuel. The growing public and political fretting over global warming has led to increased taxpayer support for biofuel subsidies, such as producing ethanol from corn, soybeans or sugar cane. This reduces the amount of corn and other foods available for human consumption and drives up the price of agri-products, as food consumers and fuel consumers compete for a limited amount of source products. This raises serious ethical concerns.

Whatever the benefits of ethanol—and they are dubious—it seems wrong to take food out of the mouths of the hungry and put it into the fuel tanks of cars in the wealthy West. There is already a backlash against biofuel subsidies.

End Malnutrition, Not Life

Much of Malthusian thinking undergirds fears of overpopulation and therefore, the thinking of those who propose anti-life policies, such as easy access to contraception, China's one-child policy, abortion as a human right and forced sterilization as corrective [to] the problem. The current concerns about rising food prices have unleashed another round of Malthusian fears. If history has taught us anything, however, it is that Malthus was wrong and his followers have been wrong time and time again.

The food price crisis will likely correct itself in time and it appears to already have begun to do so. In the meantime, instead of promoting policies to limit population growth, it would be better to solve some of the world's deadly problems, such as malaria and malnutrition. For all the fretting about food prices, the Copenhagen Consensus, a Denmark think tank that looks at world issues and prioritizes the best way to address them given a set budget, has determined that for a relatively modest $300 million, the problem of malnutrition could be addressed on a large scale.

In their contribution to the Copenhagen Consensus's *Solutions for the World's Biggest Problems: Costs and Benefits*, Jere R. Berhman and his colleagues note that "severe hunger episodes" such as famine (and presumably crises such as rapid, widespread food price increases) garner press attention, while the problem of chronic malnutrition receives little fanfare.

About a billion people are affected by malnutrition—it limits physical and mental development, kills about 600,000 children a year and limits the productivity of those who make it to adulthood. To ensure that people have sufficient food to provide them with the "energy and nutrients for fully productive lives," a relatively modest investment of $300 million would allow micro-nutrients such as iron, zinc and Vitamin A to be added to flour and other staples. That would eliminate childhood deaths from malnutrition and cost only a fraction of what the United States, for example, is spending subsidizing ethanol production.

The world does not need fear-mongering. It does however need more realism and a greater understanding of how the world works. More important, it needs to not fall victim to well-articulated but incorrect fears about food shortages that would lead to hasty and mistaken decisions about ideal population levels and growth rates.

Rather, rich Western countries should prioritize foreign aid to supply immediate, necessary food relief, while committing themselves to investing in micro-nutrients to address long-term health problems. Governments in the developing world must not look at their people as a liability and so promote anti-life policies such as abortion and birth control.

Malthus was wrong and so are his followers. A little knowledge about human history would lead to an understanding that human beings are our greatest resource, not our greatest threat.

Consumption by Wealthy Nations Is More of a Threat than Population Growth

George Monbiot

George Monbiot is a British author, journalist, and environmental activist. In the following selection, he points out that the world economy has grown much faster than the world population. As a result, Monbiot argues, economic growth is responsible for much more consumption of resources and damage to the environment than population growth. For example, the wealthy nations of the world have a growing demand for meat, resulting in more and more farmland being devoted to feed for livestock rather than to food for humans. The food crisis is therefore, in Monbiot's view, more a result of rich world policies and practices than of too many people.

As you read, consider the following questions:

1. Does Monbiot believe that global population will continue to grow indefinitely at the current rate?

2. Are population growth rates in the United States and United Kingdom typical of the rest of the world?

3. How much of the world's grain is eaten by livestock, according to Monbiot?

George Monbiot, "Population Growth Is a Threat. But It Pales Against the Greed of the Rich," *The Guardian*, January 29, 2008. www.guardian.co.uk. Reproduced by permission of Guardian News Service, LTD.

I cannot avoid the subject any longer. Almost every day I re-ceive a clutch of e-mails about it, asking the same question. A frightening new report has just pushed it up the political agenda: for the first time the World Food Programme is strug-gling to find the supplies it needs for emergency famine relief. So why, like most environmentalists, won't I mention the p-word? According to its most vociferous proponents (Paul and Anne Ehrlich), population is "our number one environ-mental problem". But most greens will not discuss it.

Is this sensitivity or is it cowardice? Perhaps a bit of both. Population growth has always been politically charged, and al-ways the fault of someone else. Seldom has the complaint been heard that "people like us are breeding too fast". For the prosperous clergyman Thomas Malthus, writing in 1798, the problem arose from the fecklessness of the laboring classes. Through the 19th and early 20th centuries, eugenicists warned that white people would be outbred. In rich nations in the 1970s the issue was over-emphasised, as it is the one environ-mental problem for which poor nations are largely to blame. But the question still needs to be answered. Is population re-ally our number one environmental problem?

The Optimum Population Trust (OPT) cites some shock-ing figures, produced by the UN. They show that if the global population keeps growing at its current rate, it will reach 134 trillion by 2300. But this is plainly absurd: no one expects it to happen. In 2005, the UN estimated that the world's popula-tion will more or less stabilise in 2200 at 10 billion. But a pa-per published in *Nature* last week suggests that there is an 88% chance that global population growth will end during this century.

In other words, if we accept the UN's projection, the global population will grow by roughly 50% and then stop. This means it will become 50% harder to stop runaway cli-mate change, 50% harder to feed the world, 50% harder to prevent the overuse of resources. But compare this rate of increase with the rate of economic growth.

Population growth has always been politically charged, and always the fault of someone else. Seldom has the complaint been heard that 'people like us are breeding too fast.'

Many economists predict that, occasional recessions notwithstanding, the global economy will grow by about 3% a year this century. Governments will do all they can to prove them right. A steady growth rate of 3% means a doubling of economic activity every 23 years. By 2100, in other words, global consumption will increase by about 1,600%. As the equations produced by Professor Roderick Smith of Imperial College have shown, this means that in the 21st century we will have used 16 times as many economic resources as human beings have consumed since we came down from the trees.

So economic growth this century could be 32 times as big an environmental issue as population growth. And if governments, banks and businesses have their way, it never stops. By 2115, the cumulative total rises to 3,200%, by 2138 to 6,400%. As resources are finite, this is of course impossible, but it is not hard to see that rising economic—not human numbers—is the immediate and overwhelmingly threat.

Those who emphasise the dangers of population growth maintain that times have changed: they are not concerned only with population growth in the poor world, but primarily with growth in the rich world, where people consume much more. The OPT maintains that the "global environmental impact of an inhabitant of Bangladesh . . . will increase by a factor of 16 if he or she emigrates to the USA". This is surely not quite true, as recent immigrants tend to be poorer than the native population, but the general point stands: population growth in the rich world, largely driven by immigration, is more environmentally damaging than an increase in population in the poor world. In the US and the UK, their ecological impact has become another stick with which immigrants can be beaten.

But growth rates in the US and UK are atypical; even the OPT concedes that by 2050 "the population of the most developed countries is expected to remain almost unchanged, at 1.2 billion". The population of the EU 25 (the first 25 nations to join the union) is likely to decline by 7 million.

Economic growth this century could be 32 times as big an environmental issue as population growth.

This, I accept, is of little consolation to people in the UK, where the government now expects numbers to rise from 61 million to 77 million by 2050. Eighty percent of the growth here, according to the OPT, is the direct or indirect result of immigration (recent arrivals tend to produce more children). Migrationwatch UK claims that migrants bear much of the responsibility for Britain's housing crisis. A graph on its Web site suggests that without them the rate of house building in England between 1997 and 2004 would have exceeded new households by 20,000–40,000 a year.

Is this true? According to the Office for National Statistics, average net immigration to the UK between 1997 and 2004 was 153,000. Let us (generously) assume that 90% of these people settled in England, and that their household size corresponded to the average for 2004, of 2.3. This would mean that new immigrants formed 60,000 households a year. The Barker Review, commissioned by the Treasury, shows that in 2002, the nearest available year, 138,000 houses were built in England, while over the 10 years to 2000, average household formation was 196,000. This rough calculation suggests that Migrationwatch is exaggerating, but that immigration is still an important contributor to housing pressure. But even total

Livestock and the Environment

Which causes more greenhouse gas emissions, rearing cattle or driving cars?

Surprise!

According to a new report published by the United Nations Food and Agriculture Organization, the livestock sector generates more greenhouse gas emissions . . . than transport. It is also a major source of land and water degradation. . . .

With increased prosperity, people are consuming more meat and dairy products every year. Global meat production is projected to more than double from 229 million tonnes in 1999/2001 to 465 million tonnes in 2050.

FAO Newsroom,
"Livestock a Major Threat to Environment,"
November 26, 2006. www.fao.org.

population growth in England is responsible for only about 35% of the demand for homes. Most of the rest is the result of the diminishing size of households.

In the rich nations we consume three times as much meat and four times as much milk per capita as the people of the poor world.

Surely there is one respect in which the growing human population constitutes the primary threat? The amount of food the world eats bears a direct relationship to the number of mouths. After years of glut, the storerooms are suddenly empty and grain prices are rocketing. How will another 3 billion be fed?

Even here, however, population growth is not the most immediate issue: another sector is expanding much faster. The UN's Food and Agriculture Organisation expects that global meat production will double by 2050—growing, in other words, at two and a half times the rate of human numbers. The supply of meat has already trebled since 1980: farm animals now take up 70% of all agricultural land and eat one third of the world's grain. In the rich nations we consume three times as much meat and four times as much milk per capita as the people of the poor world. While human population growth is one of the factors that could contribute to a global food deficit, it is not the most urgent.

None of this means that we should forget about it. Even if there were no environmental pressures caused by population growth, we should still support the measures required to tackle it: universal sex education, universal access to contraceptives, better schooling and opportunities for poor women. Stabilising or even reducing the human population would ameliorate almost all environmental impacts. But to suggest, as many of my correspondents do, that population growth is largely responsible for the ecological crisis is to blame the poor for the excesses of the rich.

Periodical Bibliography

Ronald Bailey "Make Mine Malthus!" *Reason Magazine Online*, July 28, 2004. www.reason.com.

Ronald Bailey "Under the Spell of Malthus," *Reason Magazine*, August/September 2005.

Ronald Bailey "The World Food Crisis and Political Malthusianism," *Reason Magazine Online*, July 8, 2008. www.reason.com.

Fidel Castro "Billions Condemned to Premature Death from Hunger and Thirst," Political Affairs.net, March 30, 2007. www.politicalaffairs.net.

Jim Donnelly "Global Food Crisis," *Carleton University Magazine*, Winter 2009.

Chris Haskins "The Return of Malthus," *Prospect Magazine*, January 2008.

Colum Lynch "Growing Food Crisis Strains U.N.," *Washington Post*, May 25, 2008.

Population Growth International "How Population Growth Affects Hunger in the Developing World," August 1, 2005. www.populationaction.org.

Somini Sengupta "In Fertile India, Growth Outstrips Agriculture," *New York Times*, June 22, 2008.

Bruce Stokes "Food Is Different," *National Journal Magazine Online*, June 7, 2008. www.nationaljournal.com.

Sam Urquhart "Food Crisis, Which Crisis?" *Z Magazine*, July 2008.

Voice of America Online "Ethiopia's Population Expected to Grow by More than 100 Percent by 2050," March 8, 2006. www.voanews.com.

CHAPTER 2

Population Growth and the Environment

World Population Growth Threatens Environmental Disaster

Khalid Md. Bahauddin

Khalid Md. Bahauddin is a member of the Bangladesh Society of Environmental Scientists and is associated with Jahangirnagar University. In the following viewpoint, he argues that the growth of human population is the chief threat to the world's environment. Bahauddin says that population growth contributes to freshwater scarcity, mass animal extinctions, deforestation, and depletion of fish stocks, among other environmental problems. He argues that humans must limit population growth through family planning in order to avoid environmental catastrophe.

As you read, consider the following questions:

1. According to Bahauddin, how many animal species are known to have become extinct through human action since 1600?
2. What fraction of the earth's coastlines does the author say is covered by mangroves?
3. According to Bahauddin, what percentage of major fish stocks are overfished?

Khalid Md. Bahauddin, "Foreboding of an Environmental Disaster," *The Daily Star*, August 13, 2008. www.thedailystar.net. Reproduced by permission.

Human population growth is the primary threat to the world's environment. Each person requires energy, space and resources to survive, resulting in environmental losses. Our population is rapidly rising beyond the earth's ability to regenerate and sustain us with a reasonable quality of life. We are exceeding the carrying capacity of our planet, challenging the existence of several species, including our own.

When people think of human impacts on the environment, they often think in terms of total population and population growth. The scale of our activities depends on population, consumption and the resource or pollution impact of technologies; all three of these factors are steadily increasing.

Land and Water

Rapid urban growth can bring environmental problems for cities. With many cities growing at 4 to 5% a year, provision of clean water, sewage, electricity and roads can rarely keep up with population growth. Lack of sewage treatment leads to water pollution, eutrophication [excessive plant growth] biodiversity loss in rivers and around outlets. Water demand may lower river and groundwater levels. The International Decade for Drinking Water Supply and Sanitation (1980–90) documented the growth of those without clean water in urban Africa, rising from 28 million to 31 million; those without safe sanitation rose from 38 million to 47 million.

We have transformed half the world's land for our own uses—around 11% each for farming and forestry, 26% for pasture, and another 2 to 3% for housing, industry, services and transport. In most parts of the world, cultivated land has not expanded in line with population growth, decreasing the amount of farmland per person. The area per person has declined slowly in developed countries, from 0.65 hectares [1 hectare = 2.47 acres] in 1965, to 0.51 hectares 30 years later.

In developing countries, where population growth is faster, the area per person fell from 0.3 to 0.19 hectares over this same period.

Fresh water is crucial for survival, health, agriculture, industry, comfort and leisure. But freshwater sources are limited—there is only so much to go around: the larger the population, the less there is for each person.

In 1995, some 436 million people were already suffering water scarcity or stress, causing severe development problems. There are conflicts among farmers and between rural and urban needs, and heightening tensions between countries dependent on the same resources, such as with India and Bangladesh.

The UN's 1996 population projection has estimated that, by 2050, the projected number of people suffering water stress or scarcity will have risen to 4 billion approximately.

We lose forests at the rate of 112 million hectares each decade, an area twice the size of Kenya or France.

Animals and Plants

Most ecologists believe that human activities are causing mass extinction. Since 1600, 484 animal and 654 plant species are known to have become extinct through human actions. The total extinction of a species is drastic and irreversible, but local extinction is also serious, and far more common. The Global Biodiversity Assessment listed the major threats to biodiversity as habitat loss, fragmentation and degradation, due to the need for land for farms, dwellings, industry, services, transport and leisure. Of those species that are threatened, habitat loss affects 44% of bird species, 55% of fishes, 68% of reptiles, and 75% of mammals.

Population density is closely linked with most forms of habitat loss. A sample of non-desert countries where wildlife habitat loss has been estimated showed that the percentage loss tends to be highest where population density is highest. The top 20% of countries, ranked in terms of habitat loss, had lost an average of 85% of the original wildlife habitat. Their average population density was 189 people per square kilometre. The 20% with lowest population density had lost an average of 41% of their wildlife habitat—and their average population density was only 29 people per square kilometre.

We lose forests at the rate of 112 million hectares each decade, an area twice the size of Kenya or France. Highly populated countries such as India and China have almost come to the end of their period of deforestation and have begun to reverse forest loss. Some of the fastest rates of deforestation are found in middle-income developing countries with strong commercial logging interests (Indonesia 2.4%, the Philippines 3.5%, and Thailand 2.6%).

A number of studies have found a strong correlation between population density and deforestation rates on national levels. A recent report by the United Nations Population Fund estimated an average loss of 1.8% of forests per year between 1980–90, where the population density was 89 people per square kilometre. Areas with slower deforestation tend to have lower population density; where there are just 34 people per square kilometre, the deforestation rate was only 0.5%.

Coastlines and Reefs

High percentages of human population and activity are located on or near coasts. Coastal areas have always been important for trade, transport and defence, containing some of the densest concentrations of human population and activities today. Nearly two-fifths of the world's populations live within 150 kilometres of a coastline. A recent assessment found that over half the world's coastlines are at risk from coastal development, with over one-third at high risk. Nearly three quarters of the world's marine protected areas are similarly threat-

Scientist Paul Ehrlich Says U.S. Population Growth Is Immoral

[The United States has] over 300 million people, which makes us the third largest population. But when you factor in our consumption and the technologies we use, like SUVs, our impact on life-support systems is much higher than even China's, and certainly higher than India's, which are countries with 1.3 billion and 1.1 billion people each.

I believe it is immoral and should be illegal for people to have very large numbers of children because they are then co-opting for themselves and their children resources that should be spread elsewhere in the world. You only get a chance to get your fair share.

Katherine Miesakowski,
"Do We Need Population Control?"
Salon.com, 2008. www.salon.com.

ened. In addition, human activities over vast inland areas impact coasts and coastal waters. Much of the water pollution and sediment eroded from whole watersheds is transported to the sea.

Mangroves cover an estimated 18 million hectares of the earth's tropical coastlines, around one quarter of the total. Mangroves host unique species, and are important nurseries for commercial marine species.

It is estimated that around half of all tropical mangroves have been destroyed. The Philippines, Puerto Rico, Kenya and Liberia have lost over 70%. Major pressures are cutting for fuel wood and timber; habitat conversion for coastal development or aquaculture (often shrimp farming); and damming of rivers which alters water salinity. Other direct and indirect causes of these pressures include: population growth, tourism and resource consumption in and around coastal areas.

The world has an estimated 255,000 square kilometres of near-surface coral reefs, constituting one of the richest resources of biodiversity on the planet. A recent study estimated that 58% of the world's reefs are threatened by human activity, almost half of these seriously so. In Southeast Asia, which has very high levels of coral and fish diversity, more than 80% are potentially at risk.

The threats to coral reefs are many: overfishing, pushing fish stocks below their maximum sustainable yield; destructive fishing practices; and extraction. Water pollution from industry, sewage, fertiliser, and sediment eroded from deforested or badly farmed areas all wash into the sea, reducing light levels and physically smothering corals.

Oceans

Oceans make up seven-tenths of the planet's surface, and we use an estimated 8% of their total primary productivity. Yet we have fished up to the limits or beyond, altering the ecology of a vast range of marine species.

Assessments from 1999 found that 44% of major fish stocks have already been exploited to their maximum sustainable yield. Another 16% are overfished, meaning future catches will fall unless remedial action is taken.

We need to voluntarily limit our growth, and promote contraceptive use, before nature controls our population for us with famines, droughts, and plagues.

Pollution from oil spillages, runoff and rivers includes sewage, industrial effluents, fertilisers, pesticides and herbicides. Air pollution is the source of one-third of marine pollutants.

There are now around 50 known "dead zones" with no or low oxygen. Most of these have appeared over the last half-century, and are blamed on excessive influx of nitrogen and phosphorus from farming and sewage. The dead zone in the Gulf of Mexico is 4,144 square kilometres, doubling in size since 1993.

Preventing Disaster

We need to voluntarily limit our growth, and promote contraceptive use, before nature controls our population for us with famines, droughts and plagues. Our children's future depends on us.

How people preserve or abuse the environment largely determines whether living standards improve or deteriorate. Population growth, urban expansion, and resource exploitation do not bode well for the future. Without practicing sustainable development, humanity faces a deteriorating environment and may even invite ecological disaster.

Pakistani Population Growth Will Contribute to Global Warming

Zofeen Ebrahim

Zofeen Ebrahim is a correspondent for Inter Press Service News Agency. In the following viewpoint, he reports on Professor Khalid Rashid, a Pakistani mathematician who is concerned about the catastrophic threat of climate change. Though other scientists blame wealthier nations for the increase in emissions, Rashid feels high population growth in nations such as Pakistan is an important and often overlooked source of danger. Rashid argues that Pakistani leaders need to overcome religious objections and make birth control and family planning more easily available.

As you read, consider the following questions:

1. According to Professor Rashid, how many people will there be on the Indian subcontinent in 2050?
2. According to Ebrahim, what is Pakistan's annual growth rate?
3. According to the author, is Pakistan's fertility rate lower or higher than that of Bangladesh?

When it comes to climate change, population matters, particularly for countries in South Asia, Africa and some Arab countries, says Prof. Khalid Rashid. A mathemati-

Zofeen Ebrahim, "PAKISTAN: Uncontrolled Population Blamed for Climate Change," Inter Press Service News Agency, July 31, 2007. http://ipsnews.net. Reproduced by permission.

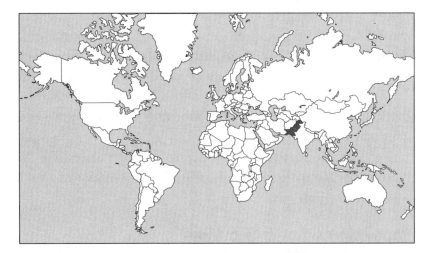

cian and physicist in Pakistan, he has long been studying the phenomenon of global warming and views the uncontrolled population explosion with much trepidation.

'Deep down, human population is the main cause. If the world population would stay around 100 million, this population could afford an energy-intensive, yet sustainable, lifestyle.'

But there are climate scientists like Dr. Shaheen Rafi Khan, a researcher with an Islamabad-based policy-oriented research institute, the Sustainable Development Policy Institute (SDPI), who insist it is how we live and use resources that matters, not the number of people.

"Because," insists Dr. Khan, "the focus remains on emissions in the North and adaptation to climate change in the South. The South is the victim of climate change, not the agent."

He, however, adds: "Population growth impact is likely to be incremental and the country that will contribute substantively to it will be India, with its large and growing population and surging economic growth."

As people struggle to survive in poor countries, environmental degradation is more pervasive. Long-term sustainable development goals are disregarded in favour of immediate subsistence needs. Increased use of wood for fuel, abusive use of land and water resources—in the form of overgrazing, overfishing, depletion of fresh water and desertification—are common in poor countries.

In Asia, in particular, another cause for concern is the rapid industrialisation of India and China. This means fossil fuel consumption has increased.

Population Growth Is a Main Cause of Climate Change

"Deep down, human population is the main cause. If the world population would stay around 100 million, this population could afford an energy-intensive, yet sustainable, lifestyle. The effect on the planet would be small," says Prof. Rashid.

The mathematician in him begins calculating. "It is very obvious that by 2050, the Indian subcontinent will have to support 350 million Pakistanis; 1.65 billion Indians; 40 million Nepalese; 300 million Bangladeshis and 30 million Sri Lankans. The total will be about 2.4 billion people. This was the total population of the whole earth around 1950. The strain on resources will be tremendous, and consequences catastrophic," he prophesies.

By then the glaciers in the Himalayas will be gone, the monsoons will be erratic, sometimes too much or too little rain; new uncontrollable diseases will have emerged, he adds. "We are headed for a mega disaster. It will come overnight. We will wake up, and find that all we had yesterday (food, water, electricity) are gone," the professor concludes.

The world's population is projected to increase by 40 percent in 2050. Pakistan, with an annual growth rate of 2.69 percent, as given in the government's Statistical Year Book 2006, will be the sixth most populous country.

Population Drives Global Warming

Since 1950, the number of people in the world has surged from 2.5 billion to more than 6.2 billion. At the same time, carbon dioxide and other gases in the atmosphere have risen as people use more fossil fuel, produce more chemicals, and cut down more forests. As a result, average global temperature has climbed. The 1990s were the warmest decade in the 20th century; 1998, 2001 and 2005 were the hottest years on record. There is wide agreement that this will accelerate if current trends persist.

Earth Day Network,
"Global Climate Change and Population," 2008.
http://earthday.net.

Birth Control Is Unpopular

There seems to be no stopping the runaway growth here because birth control is often portrayed as anti-people. The subject is not broached. The country's political and religious leaders who could make a difference are to blame.

"They have ignored the explosive population growth completely. Birth control is a taboo topic. In our culture, the larger the number of children, the stronger the family feels. Poverty does not seem to matter," says Prof. Rashid. "The mullahs (clerics) may not like it!" adds Dr. Khan.

The rural population has been kept illiterate in Pakistan, he declares. "Instead of building schools we built armies. The feudal landowners saw to it that the rural population is kept away from schooling. Many of the Ulema [Muslim regal scholars] declare girls' education to be un-Islamic," Prof. Rashid explains.

The reality is that even where women want fewer children or practice birth spacing they face difficulty in accessing the family planning services. They meet with a non-supportive environment at home and encounter misconceptions and misinformation about the use of family planning.

'Birth control is a taboo topic. In our culture, the larger the number of children, the stronger the family feels. Poverty does not seem to matter.'

In addition, Pakistan has a very young population with an extremely high fertility—much higher, for instance, than Bangladesh or Thailand. This young population will soon become adults and come into the reproductive age. And even if there is a decline in average fertility to the reproductive level (of 2.1 children per woman) by 2020, Pakistan will still have a population of 350 million by 2050, according to the UN [United Nations] medium variant projection.

Dr. Khan appeals to Pakistan's leaders to tackle the population growth issue, also "because of its climate change implications. Urban emissions pose huge health hazards in southern cities. They are directly related to burgeoning urban populations thanks to high fertility and rural-urban drift."

Unfortunately green lobbyists everywhere have shied away from the issue, according to Dr. Khan. They are more concerned about the impact on biodiversity, he points out.

Dr. R.K. Pachauri, chairman of the Intergovernmental Panel on Climate Change (IPCC), while agreeing that a larger population will cause greater emissions of greenhouse gases (GHGs) which causes climate change, feels a still more important question is: "how population encroaches on biodiversity resources?"

Dr. Kashif M. Sheikh, a biodiversity specialist, concludes: "Exponential human growth is the greatest challenge not only to biodiversity but to sustaining and conserving biodiversity in all its lives and forms."

Dr. Khan, however does not subscribe to the theory that massive growth in population has had more impact on biodiversity than any other single factor. "No, recent research shows a tenuous population-poverty-degradation nexus. The problem lies in management and giving people their resource rights," he insists.

Australia Faces Water Shortages as Population Grows

Luke Sunner

Luke Sunner is a writer for Alluvium Consulting, an Australian water resource management consulting firm. In the following viewpoint, he writes about Queensland, a state in the northeast of Australia, many parts of which are experiencing extreme water shortages. Sunner says that the water shortages are caused by a number of factors, including drought, climate change, and population growth. Queensland is one of the fastest growing states in Australia. When population increase is combined with poor water-use habits, Sunner argues, shortages follow. Sunner points out that Queensland has instituted many policies to deal with the threat, including water restrictions and use of recycled water. Sunner also says that individuals can help by conserving water.

As you read, consider the following questions:

1. According to Sunner, from April 2006 to March 2007, water flowing into Queensland's three main supply dams was what percentage of the average water flow?

2. According to Sunner, what are some of the poor water-use attitudes or practices of the general public?

Luke Sunner, "We Are All a Part of the Solution," Alluvium Consulting Editorials, October 12, 2007. www.alluvium.com.au. Reproduced by permission.

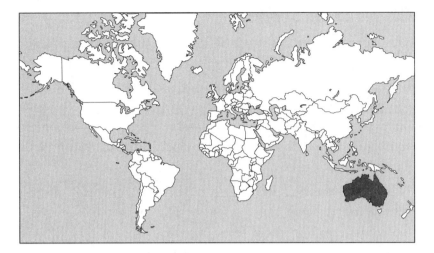

3. What does Sunner say is the most environmentally costly water supply solution?

The combination of the worst drought ever recorded, a legacy of poor water resource practices, the variability of climate change and a steadily growing population has resulted in huge demands on water supplies. This is a statement that could probably be applied to all states and territories in Australia. But here's a view of the situation in Queensland.

Many parts of Queensland are currently experiencing the effects of prolonged drought. In particular South East Queensland is currently experiencing its worst drought in more than 100 years; water flowing into dams and other storages throughout the region is at lowest ever recorded levels[5]. Between April 2006 and March 2007, water flowing into the three main water supply dams (North Pine, Wivenhoe and Somerset) for South East Queensland was less than 5 percent of the normal average[5]. Figure 1 [not shown] shows the trend in dam water levels as a percentage of total capacity over the last few years and as of October 8, 2007 the total storage level of the three main dams combined was 21.06% of total capacity[10].

Causes of the Shortage

The current water supply situation in South East Queensland is not caused by any one factor alone; it is the result of a multitude of contributing factors. Arguably, some of the most prominent factors leading to the current situation are: reliance on existing traditional surface water storages as the main source of supply, drought, climate change, population growth, and poor water use/consumption attitudes of society.

Out of these contributing factors drought and climate change are the two most unpredictable with the least scope for control and/or short-term change. A recent report titled *Climate Change in Australia*[3] predicts Australia will generally become increasingly hotter and drier. In eastern Australia, towards the middle and latter stages of this century, it is expected that there will be an increase in the number of drought months and evaporation. It is therefore most likely that the catchments of the three major supply dams, [Wivenhoe, Somerset, and North Pine] will yield less water in the future. This is an alarming concept given over 75% of water used throughout South East Queensland is supplied from these three traditional surface water storages[8].

Queensland is widely known throughout Australia as one of the fastest growing states. Since the 1980s South East Queensland has sustained steady population growth, with an average increase of 55,300 persons per year from 1986 to 2004[11]. When these factors are combined with poor water use/consumption attitudes and practices of the general public, such as:

- Maintaining water thirsty household gardens and lawns

- Use of sprinklers

- Washing concrete and paved areas

- Taking lengthy showers

- Washing cars in the driveway

- Not turning off taps

- Dripping taps

- Use of water-inefficient household appliances

It is not surprising to see the south east of Queensland under the grip of a water supply shortage with the community living with government-imposed water restrictions since 13 May 2005[9].

Since the 1980s South East Queensland has sustained steady population growth, with an average increase of 55,300 persons per year from 1986 to 2004.

What Is Being Done?

With the population of South East Queensland set to increase from 2.46 million in 2001 to 3.71 million people in 2026[11], the government and society face a significant challenge to ensure water supplies are secure from drought into the future. How is this challenge being met?

Unfortunately this is a complex problem, meaning the solution is likely to be just as complex with no simple 'fix-all' solutions. In response to this the Queensland Government is implementing the largest urban drought response in Australia[5] to create a portfolio of water supply solutions, which it says will ensure a healthy future for the Queensland economy and Queenslanders. The portfolio includes:

- Desalination

- Recycled water through advanced wastewater treatment plants

- Pipelines

- New dams

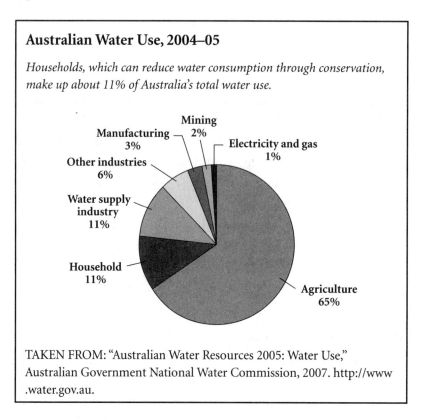

Australian Water Use, 2004–05

Households, which can reduce water consumption through conservation, make up about 11% of Australia's total water use.

Mining 2%
Manufacturing 3%
Electricity and gas 1%
Other industries 6%
Water supply industry 11%
Household 11%
Agriculture 65%

TAKEN FROM: "Australian Water Resources 2005: Water Use," Australian Government National Water Commission, 2007. http://www .water.gov.au.

- Groundwater extraction

- Rainwater tanks and storm water harvesting

- Improved network efficiency

- Regulation with water restrictions and penalties

- Other conservation initiatives (including rebate schemes) aimed at reducing household water use in South East Queensland to 140 litres per person per day[5][7].

Each of these projects/programs have their advantages and costs to the economy, society and the environment. Perhaps the most costly to the environment would be the installation of new dams. At the third International Symposium on Riverine Landscapes held at Griffith University's Australian Rivers

Institute earlier this year [2007], Professor Stuart Bunn commented that the greatest threat to waterways are human water use, land use impacts and climate change. He added that rivers are regarded as the most threatened ecosystems on the planet and global population growth and water demand are causing unprecedented changes to river systems[1]. With this in mind it is evident there is increasing environmental concern over new large surface water storages implying the scope for new surface water storage projects into the future is set to reduce[4].

Using South East Queensland as an example, the simplest and most cost effective solution lies with changing our water use attitudes and practicing conservation at home and at work.

Conservation Is the Best Solution

On the other side of the coin, so to speak, in an urban environment, water conservation is the most environmentally friendly water shortage solution, reducing demand from the various water sources. Until recently water has been treated as an endless resource by many, wasting copious quantities of this precious resource. In South East Queensland water use habits and attitudes of society are changing during this time of drought. Currently, household water usage in South East Queensland has been significantly reduced to approximately 130 litres per person per day[6] (or 47.5 KL/person/year) achieving massive water savings. This compares to an approximate average household consumption of 342 litres per person per day (or 125 KL/person/year) in Queensland for the year 2004–05[2].

Drought affects many Queensland communities and the Queensland Government is implementing a number of projects in response to this. Is the government doing enough to secure our future water supplies? Who knows? However, we are all a part of the solution and together have the power to significantly influence the security of our own water supplies before water supplies turn into supply crises. Using South East Queensland as an example, the simplest and most cost effective solution lies with changing our water use attitudes and practicing conservation at home and at work.

References

1. ABC, 2007. Scientists hold summit on saving world's rivers [online], Available from: http://www.abc.net.au/news/stories/2007/08/28/2017187.htm?site=water

2. Commonwealth of Australia, 2005. Capital City Water Use [online], Available from: http://www.water.gov.au/WaterUse/Capitalcitywateruse/index.aspx?Menu=Level1_4_3

3. CSIRO & Australian Bureau of Meteorology, 2007. Climate change in Australia: technical report 2007, CSIRO, 148 pp.

4. Hanak, E, 2007. Finding Water for Growth: New Sources, New Tools, New Challenges, Journal of the American Water Resources Association (JAWRA) 43(4): 1024–1035. DOI: 10.11/j. 17527–1688. 2007. 00084.x

5. Queensland Government, 2007. Water for the future [online Available from: http://www.infrastructure.qld.gov.au/library/txt/Water_for_the_future_june07.txt

6. Queensland Water Commission, 2007. Individual Daily Water Usage [online], Available from: http://www.target140.com.au/

7. Queensland Water Commission, 2007. Projects and planning [online], Available from: http://www.qwc.qld.gov.au/Planning+and+reform

8. Queensland Water Commission, 2007. Water Resources [online], Available from: http://www.qwc.qld.gov.au/Water+resources

9. Queensland Water Commission, 2007. Water restrictions [online], Available from: http://www.qwc.qld.gov.au/Water+restrictions

10. SEQ Water, 2007. Dam Operations & Maintenance [online], Available from: http://www.seqwater.com.au/content/standard.asp?name=DamOperationsAndMaintenance

11. The State of Queensland (Department of Infrastructure), 2007. South East Queensland Regional Plan–Part B: Growth Management [online], Available from: http://www.dip.qld.gov.au/seq

Indonesia Fisheries May Be Destroyed as Population Grows

WALHI, the Indonesian Forum for Environment

WALHI, the Indonesian Forum for Environment is dedicated to defending Indonesia's environment and its local communities from exploitative economic development. In the following viewpoint, the organization argues that population growth in Indonesia is exceeding fisheries production. WALHI claims that if this continues, there will be a collapse of fish stocks. Some types of fish will become unavailable, and others will become prohibitively expensive. In order to prevent this, WALHI says that Indonesia must crack down on illegal fishing and stop exporting fish.

As you read, consider the following questions:

1. In the five years before this article was written, how many tons of fish was consumed in Indonesia?
2. What fish species has been lost in the waters of Bengkalis Island?
3. According to WALHI, for how long should Indonesia cease exporting fish?

Politics and fisheries policy that are focused on export activities are no longer relevant or appropriate now that Indonesian population growth has exceeded national fisheries

WALHI, the Indonesian Forum for Environment, "The Indonesian Fisheries Crisis," March 26, 2007. www.walhi.or.id. Reproduced by permission.

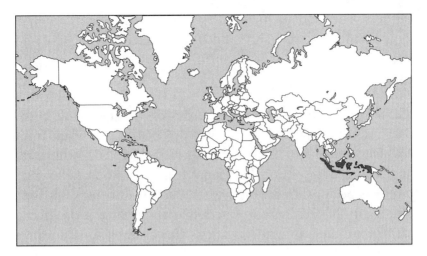

production. Fisheries policy that focuses on the availability of imports must be given over in view of the fact that domestic fisheries are experiencing a decline in potential catch.

In the last 5 years, [2002–2007] national fish consumption jumped to more than 1.2 million tons, together with a growth in the Indonesian population of 1.34% per year. It is not surprising that the value of national fisheries imports has increased by 12.51% (2004–2005)...

It is undeniable that within 8 years, there will be an increase [worldwide] in demand for fish and fisheries products of 50 million tons.

In view of the population growth in Indonesia, the pattern of national fish consumption can be expected to gradually rise. National fish consumption is currently about 26 kg per capita per year. If not managed properly, it is quite possible that we will suffer a fisheries crisis.

Abundant marine potential combined with the extent of our seas means that a fisheries crisis should not occur if fisheries policies have appropriate targets. A crisis will only occur if there is inappropriate exploitation of available marine resources. The fundamental and predominant problems are then how to manage, revitalize and utilize fisheries in a wise and sustainable way.

Approaching Crisis

Currently, Indonesia's marine fisheries are capturing 60 to 70% of the total available potential. This data is taken from the Department of Seas and Fisheries (DKP-RI), who state that about 60% or so of national fisheries resource distribution has been utilized. However, this seems to be at odds with the reality of archipelago waters that show: first, a decline in the fishing catch in many locations (for example, in the waters of Bitung-North Sulawesi, Tanjung Balai-North Sumatra, Bengkalis-Riau, Lampung Bay, etc.); second, a decrease in the raw materials that support the fisheries industry. There is no way to misconstrue that, by 2006, four fisheries in North Sulawesi were forced to halt production due to the scarcity of raw materials; and three, the loss of certain fish species, such as shad (terubuk) in Bengkalis Island, Riau.

In reality, the fisheries crisis is not just a national trend. Rather, the FAO [Food and Agriculture Organization] predicts an ongoing rise in total global demand for fish and fisheries products. This is associated with growth in the global population ... and increase in global fish consumption, which has already reached 19 kg per capita per year. It is undeniable that within 8 years, there will be an increase in demand for fish and fisheries products of 50 million tons. Rather than being able to meet this demand, the availability of global fisheries resources is already experiencing a deficit of 9–10 million tons per year.

Solutions

In order to economize and transform fisheries, holistic policy measures need to be taken.

First, re-strengthening the role of state (state building) through eradication of illegal fishing activities (administrative

---

World Fisheries Are Predicted to Collapse

All species of wild seafood that are currently fished are projected to collapse by the year 2050, according to a new four year study by an international team of ecologists and economists. Collapse is defined as 90 percent depletion.

The scientists warn that the loss of biodiversity is "profoundly" reducing the ocean's ability to produce seafood, resist diseases, filter pollutants, and rebound from stresses such as overfishing and climate change.

"Whether we looked at tide pools or studies over the entire world's ocean, we saw the same picture emerging," says lead author Boris Worm of Dalhousie University. "In losing species we lose the productivity and stability of entire ecosystems. I was shocked and disturbed by how consistent these trends are—beyond anything we suspected."

Environmental News Service,
"Collapse of All Wild Fisheries Predicted in 45 Years,"
2006. www.ens-newswire.com.

---

infringements, catch route infringements, and use of destructive catch tools). The results of verification by the DKP Director-General for Fisheries (March 2006) showed that 94% of ship fisheries certificates that were successfully verified were false. At least 1.5 million ton/year fish are taken from Indonesian waters as a consequence of illegal fishing. Like it or not, the government has to be more persistent in combating illegal fishing practices, which cost the country some US $4 billion.

Second, a stop of export activities for the next 10–15 years. This hiatus is needed because national consumption is predicted to increase and the quantity demanded will be unprocurable for local consumption if fisheries export activities are allowed to continue. Data on the fisheries trade balance published by the DKP indicates an increase in exports each year. The country receives more than US $1.7 million in export value [as of 2004] from fisheries export activities. This indicates that about 1 million tons of fish are allocated to meet global fish consumption needs, in addition to the allocation from illegal fishing activities.

Still Time to Act

In the next 10 years, the unfolding fisheries crisis in Indonesia is certain to destroy our fisheries resources. At this stage of the crisis, we have begun to experience increasing difficulty in finding particular fish species in the marketplace, both local and global, and increasing prices for fish beyond normal thresholds.

In view of this, the government must pioneer the revitalisation of our fisheries' potential by focusing on satisfying the national demand while at the same time re-evaluating the remaining fisheries resources. Externally, the government must close the tap on fisheries exports, by taking diplomatic initiatives to garner international support. Internally, illegal fishing practices need to be addressed as a fundamental priority. This program would entail improving the mechanism for issuing permits and developing a professional and transparent judicial system for fisheries.

It is still possible for President Susilo Bambang Yudhoyono (and his cabinet), in the time remaining, to involve fishermen and the wider community in efforts to overcome and withstand the national fisheries crisis, which is unfolding right in front of our eyes.

Asia's Population and Economic Growth Has Created Serious Pollution Problems

Gretchen Cook-Anderson

Gretchen Cook-Anderson works for the National Aeronautics and Space Administration. In this viewpoint, Cook-Anderson discusses the results of a pollution migration pattern study using measurements taken by the Moderate Resolution Imaging Spectroradiometer (MODIS) instrument on NASA's Terra satellite over the last seven years. According to the study, the rising population and economic growth in China has resulted in a doubling of its emissions of man-made pollutants. About 10 billion pounds of pollutants per year reached North America from Asia during the period of the study.

As you read, consider the following questions:

1. According to the study, how much pollution was exported from Asia out over the Pacific Ocean?

2. What percentage of the local North American pollution does the Asian pollution export amount to?

3. According to the study, what other region is a source of pollutants arriving in North America?

Gretchen Cook-Anderson, "NASA Satellite Measures Pollution from East Asia to North America," NASA's Goddard Space Flight Center. www.nasa.gov.

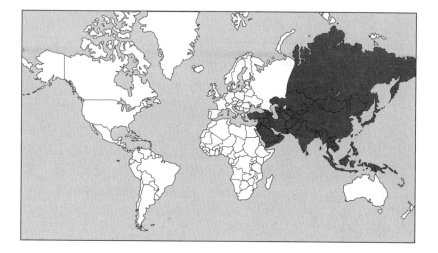

In a new NASA study, researchers taking advantage of improvements in satellite sensor capabilities offer the first measurement-based estimate of the amount of pollution from East Asian forest fires, urban exhaust, and industrial production that makes its way to western North America.

China, the world's most populated country, has experienced rapid industrial growth, massive human migrations to urban areas, and considerable expansion in automobile use over the last two decades. As a result, the country has doubled its emissions of man-made pollutants to become the world's largest emitter of tiny particles called pollution aerosols that are transported across the Pacific Ocean by rapid airstreams emanating from East Asia.

Hongbin Yu, an associate research scientist of the University of Maryland Baltimore County working at NASA's Goddard Space Flight Center in Greenbelt, Md., grew up in China and taught there as a university professor, where he witnessed first-hand and studied how pollution from nearby power plants in China affected the local environment. Early this decade, scientists began using emerging high-accuracy satellite data to answer key questions about the role tiny particles play in the atmosphere, and eventually expanded their research to include continent-to-continent pollution transport. So Yu teamed with other researchers to take advantage of the innovations in satellite technology and has now made the first-ever satellite-based estimate of pollution aerosols transported from East Asia to North America.

The new measurements from the Moderate Resolution Imaging Spectroradiometer (MODIS) instrument on NASA's Terra satellite substantiate the results of previous model-based studies, and are the most extensive to date. The new study will be published this spring in the American Geophysical Union's Journal of Geophysical Research-Atmospheres.

"We used the latest satellite capabilities to distinguish industrial pollution and smoke from dust transported to the western regions of North America from East Asia. Looking at four years of data from 2002 to 2005 we estimated the amount of pollution arriving in North America to be equivalent to about 15 percent of local emissions of the U.S. and Canada," Yu said. "This is a significant percentage at a time when the U.S. is trying to decrease pollution emissions to boost overall air quality. This means that any reduction in our emissions may be offset by the pollution aerosols coming from East Asia and other regions."

Yu and his colleagues measured the trans-Pacific flow of pollution in teragrams, a unit of measurement of the mass of pollution aerosol (1 teragram is about 2.2 billion pounds). Satellite data confirmed 18 teragrams—almost 40 billion pounds—of pollution aerosol was exported to the northwestern Pacific Ocean and 4.5 teragrams nearly 10 billion pounds—reached North America annually from East Asia over the study period.

Yu points out, however, that the matter of pollution transport is a global one. "Our study focused on East Asian pollution transport, but pollution also flows from Europe, North America, the broader Asian region and elsewhere, across bodies of water and land, to neighboring areas and beyond," he said. "So we should not simply blame East Asia for this amount of pollution flowing into North America." In fact, in a model study published last November in the Journal of Atmospheric Chemistry and Physics, Mian Chin, also a co-author of this study and an atmospheric scientist at NASA Goddard, suggests that European pollution also makes a significant contribution to the pollution inflow to North America.

Notably, the pollution aerosols also travel quickly. They cross the ocean and journey into the atmosphere above North American in as little as one week.

"Satellite instruments give us the ability to capture more accurate measurements, on a nearly daily basis across a broader geographic region and across a longer time frame so that the overall result is a better estimate than any other measurement method we've had in the past," said study co-author Lorraine Remer, a physical scientist and member of the MODIS science team at NASA Goddard. The MODIS instrument can distinguish between broad categories of particles in the air, and observes Earth's entire surface every one to two days, enabling it to monitor movement of the East Asian pollution aerosols as they rise into the lower troposphere, the area of the atmosphere where we live and breathe, and make their way across the Pacific and up into the middle and upper regions of the troposphere.

Remer added that the research team also found that pollution movements fluctuate during the year, with the East Asian airstream carrying its largest "load" in spring and smallest in summer. The most extensive East Asian export of pollution across the Pacific took place in 2003, triggered by record-breaking wildfires across vast forests of East Asia and Russia. Notably, the pollution aerosols also travel quickly. They cross the ocean and journey into the atmosphere above North American in as little as one week.

"Using this imaging instrument, we cannot determine at what level of elevation in the atmosphere pollution travels. So, we do not have a way in this study to assess the degree of impact the pollution aerosols from China have on air quality here once they cross over to North America. We need improved technology to make that determination," said Remer. "Nevertheless, we realize there is indeed impact. For example, particles like these have been linked to regional weather and climate effects through interactions between pollution aerosols and the Sun's heat energy. Since pollution transport is such a broad global issue, it is important moving forward to extend this kind of study to other regions, to see how much pollution is migrating from its source regions to others, when, and how fast," said Remer.

According to measurements taken with a satellite instrument, vast quantities of industrial aerosols and smoke from biomass burning in East Asia and Russia are traveling from one side of the globe to another. Explosive economic growth in Asia has profound implications for the atmosphere worldwide. Data collected by a NASA satellite shows a dense blanket of polluted air over the Northwestern Pacific. This brown cloud is a toxic mix of ash, acids, and airborne particles from car and factory emissions, as well as from low-tech polluters like coal-burning stoves and from forest fires. [The] image generated by data from NASA's instrument called MODIS (Moderate Resolution Imaging Spectroradiometer) onboard the Terra satellite demonstrates how large and pervasive this transport phenomenon is across vast areas.

In [the] picture [generated from data from MODIS, not available here], heavy aerosol concentrations appear in shades of brown, with darker shades representing greater concentrations. Areas lined in black on the land surface represent human population. Notice how heavy aerosol production and dense population areas correspond. Also notice how there are dense patches of red points in East Asia. These correspond

An Explosion in Car Ownership in China

In 1990 there were just one million cars on Chinese roads. Fourteen years later that number has rapidly risen to 12 million, and this year [2007] alone a further 2.4 million new cars will be added. In itself, that's a lot of new cars, but the figures take on an altogether greater significance when you realise where this trend might lead.

Currently China still only has eight vehicles per thousand residents, whereas Brazil has 122, countries in Western Europe have an average of 584, and in the US there are a massive 940 cars for every thousand residents. As Chinese environmentalist Liang Congjie says: 'If each Chinese family has two cars like US families, then the cars needed by China, something like 600 million vehicles, will exceed all the cars in the world combined. That would be the greatest disaster for mankind.'

Yves Engler and Bianca Mugyenyi,
"China's Cars on Road to Ruin,"
Peopleandplanet.net, 2005. www.peopleandplanet.net.

with intense forest fires, sending vast quantities of aerosols into the atmosphere. Although this image gives the impression that the fires and plumes of aerosols may not be connected, in fact they are. There's a direct relationship between those fire points and the brown patches appearing to the East.

China's exports fill shelves around the world, but according to a new NASA research paper, China also heavily exports pollution. This week, space agency scientists reveal how Chinese industrialization and Russian forest fires in combination with pollution transported eastward from Europe send roughly 18 teragrams almost 40 billion pounds of pollution aerosols into the atmosphere over the Northwestern Pacific every year. The MODIS instrument on NASA's Terra satellite has been tracking the particulate pollution for more than seven years, gathering data as most of it drifted east across the Pacific Ocean. About 4.5 teragrams of particulate pollution each year could reach the western boundary of North America, which is about 15% of local emissions of particulate pollutants from the U.S. and Canada.

In the last two decades, China has more than doubled its pollution production. This boom may be contributing to substantial changes in climate and weather in places far from the origin of the particulates. Never in human history anywhere has there been industrial growth like that in modern China. But with fast growth comes unintended consequences, and from space evidence of those consequences is starting to emerge.

The research relies on measurements of something called "aerosol optical thickness". It's a quantitative measurement about how well a slice of atmosphere transmits light. The greater the value of optical thickness for a given location, the less light of a particular wavelength can pass through it. Measurements of aerosol optical thickness describe quantities of tiny particles in a given volume. By measuring how much light can penetrate a region of atmosphere across a variety of wavelengths, scientists can make certain inferences about the quantity and type of particles blocking that light.

[The MODIS] visualization shows the seasonal variations of transport of pollution aerosols across the North Pacific. The East Asian airstream carries its largest pollution loading in spring and smallest in summer and fall. With heavy concentrations of aerosols represented by shades of brown, scientists can track the origins and distribution of the particles as they travel in the atmosphere. The sequence also shows a trail of substantial aerosol concentrations from a variety of sources. These sources include heavy industrial activity in East Asia associated with high population density represented in this sequence by gradations of black covering the land surface, and intense Russian forest fires in high latitudes.

The Galapagos Islands Face Loss of Ecological Treasures as Population Grows

Galapagos Conservancy

The Galapagos Conservancy is the largest private organization devoted to conserving the Galapagos, an archipelago, or group of islands, off the coast of Ecuador. The archipelago is famous for its diverse and unique animal life. In the following viewpoint, the Conservancy points out that the human population on the Galapagos Islands has exploded since 1991. The increase in population has been caused mostly by immigration, as people from the economically poor mainland of Ecuador move to the islands to take advantage of a booming tourist industry and, to a lesser extent, of a healthy fishing industry. The growth in population requires more infrastructure—airports, fuel, roads—which can damage animal habitat. Population growth also increases the likelihood that non-native, or invasive, species will manage to establish themselves on the islands. Non-native mammals, birds, and plants can drive out and destroy native species, radically altering the Galapagos Islands' unique ecology.

As you read, consider the following questions:

1. Who wrote *The Voyage of the Beagle*, one of the early accounts of the Galapagos Islands?

Galapagos Conservancy, "Human Presence" and "Invasive Species," Galapagos Conservancy, 2008. www.galapagos.org. Reproduced by permission.

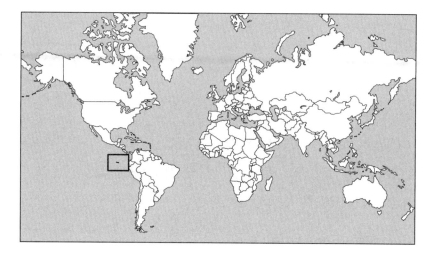

2. During the 1990s, what percentage of Ecuadorians fled their country?

3. According to the Galapagos Conservancy, what is the greatest environmental threat to the Galapagos?

The Galapagos Islands developed in isolation since they emerged from the sea a few million years ago, but this isolation has been eroding ever since their discovery in 1535. For over 400 years man has had an influence on the archipelago's ecosystems and evolutionary processes.

As early as the mid 1600s, buccaneers used the islands as a base from which to attack mainland ports and sea routes used to transport valuables along the coast. From the 1700s to the mid 1800s, whalers used the islands as a base to hunt the rich waters to the west of the archipelago, while fur sealers harvested the valuable pelts of the Galapagos fur seal. Slowly the archipelago became better known to the world, through the maps of privateers such as William Dampier, whalers such as James Colnett, and the accounts of Charles Darwin in his book, *The Voyage of the Beagle.* Annexed by Ecuador in 1832, the islands were subsequently used for agriculture, fishing, incarcerating criminals, harvesting of Orchilla—lichen—and harvesting and processing of giant tortoises for their oil. During the Second World War, the government of Ecuador allowed the United States to use the island of Baltra as a military base.

Despite this long history of human interaction with Galapagos, population growth remained relatively slow up until the early 1970s, at which time residents numbered approximately 4,000. Since that time a combination of factors has lead to a process of rapid and sustained growth.

Since its beginnings in the 1960s, tourism has been the most important factor contributing to population growth.

Between 1991 and 2007, the resident population more than doubled. The population stands at 24,000 legal residents, 1,800 temporary residents and up to 5,000 residents whose status in Galapagos is characterized as "irregular."

Causes of Rapid Population Growth

Galapagos tourism. Since its beginnings in the 1960s, tourism has been the most important factor contributing to population growth. Over the past 15 years, gross income generated by tourism has increased by an average of 14% each year. This growth is reflected in the increase in available beds (in both hotels and on tourist boats) from 1,928 in 1991 to 3,473 in 2006 and the rise in the number of visitors to Galapagos from 40,000 in 1990 to more than 145,000 in 2006. At present, Galapagos tourism generates $418M annually, of which an estimated $63M enters the local economy (equal to 51% of the Galapagos economy). The growth in tourism requires ever-increasing infrastructure and human resources. It has also resulted in the growth of local small enterprises, which, in turn, contribute to increased immigration.

Poor economic conditions on mainland Ecuador. During the 1980s and 1990s, Ecuador faced declining oil prices (its primary export) and costly border issues with Peru and Colombia. Between 1981 and 1991, the Sucre, the national currency at the time, lost 98% of its value. Real per capita income eroded, inflation was out of control, and bank interest rates topped 70%. By the year 2000, 9.5 million of the country's 13.5 million inhabitants lived below the poverty level. These conditions caused an exodus of Ecuadorians. According to the Ecuadorian newspaper *El Comercio*, during the 1990s alone, between 15–20% of the nation's residents fled the country. While most sought to establish themselves in Spain and the United States, others chose not to flee the country but instead relocate in Galapagos, one of the few bright spots in the beleaguered national economy.

Other Factors in Growth

International demand for marine species. Although local fisheries have played a much smaller part in the Galapagos economy than tourism and some other activities, in the early to mid 1990s, the high international price for sea cucumbers and the initial abundance of this species in Galapagos provided another economic incentive for migration from the mainland. Today fishing represents only 4% of the Galapagos economy but has a much larger social and political impact.

Public sector investments and subsidies. The Ecuadorian government began to make significant expenditures in public and institutional infrastructure during Ecuador's oil boom (1972–1983). It also established transportation, energy, and public sector salary subsidies because of the archipelago's isolation and the fact that it was considered a hardship area for residents and public sector employees. Public works programs and administrative positions lured immigrants during an era jokingly referred to as "the bureaucratization of Galapagos." On a per capita basis, the islands continue to receive more government funding than any of the nation's other provinces.

Growth in Galapagos

This chart shows growing population and growing tourism on Galapagos. Note that human population figures are on the left, visitors are on the right. The graph scale has to be split like this because the number of visitors is so much greater than the number of permanent residents.

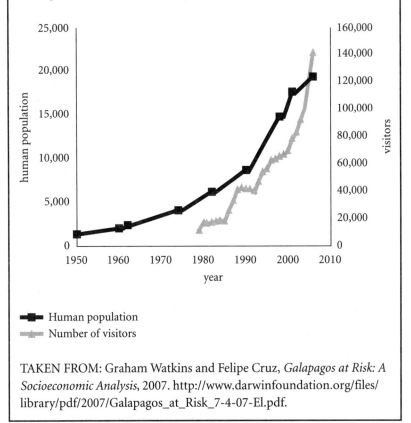

■ Human population
▲ Number of visitors

TAKEN FROM: Graham Watkins and Felipe Cruz, *Galapagos at Risk: A Socioeconomic Analysis*, 2007. http://www.darwinfoundation.org/files/library/pdf/2007/Galapagos_at_Risk_7-4-07-El.pdf.

Improvements in infrastructure and public services, combined with ongoing subsidies, have made the islands an increasingly desirable place to live.

Impacts of Population Growth

In the larger protected areas and at visitor sites, the impact of increased numbers of visitors and residents has been fairly well managed through standard protected area management techniques, including trails, guides to accompany visitors, fixed itineraries, and a limited number of tourism concessions. The Galapagos National Park Service monitors visitor sites and can close sites, increase necessary infrastructure such as stairs or walkways, or change itineraries in response to growing pressures.

The impacts in the inhabited portions of the archipelago have been much more pronounced. Increasing numbers of visitors and residents have resulted in a rapid growth in physical infrastructure and ever-increasing demands for public services.

The good news is that 95% of the archipelago's native species remain intact today, due in large part to the islands' remoteness. . . . However, it is the island's isolation that makes the native plants and animals so vulnerable to new arrivals.

As the human population in Galapagos has grown, the number of airports in the islands has increased from one to three, the number of flights from the continent have increased from a few flights per week in the 1970s to an average of six flights per day today, the number of cargo ships and the amount of cargo continue to increase, and increasingly more fuel is brought to the islands, increasing the risk of oil spills such as that of the cargo ship Jessica in 2001. Commercial flights to Galapagos increased by 193% from 2001 to 2006 and more private flights are arriving from other countries. New access routes overcome natural barriers that protect the islands from the arrival of new species. Any increase in flights, new access routes, and cargo ships will potentially bring an increasing number of invasive species—the greatest threat to the archipelago. . . .

Invasive Species

Scientists and conservationists agree that introduced plants and animals represent the single greatest threat to the terrestrial ecosystems of Galapagos. Since the discovery of Galapagos in 1535, humans have brought many alien species to the islands—some intentionally, including goats, pigs, cats, and both ornamental and food plants (vegetables and fruits), to name a few—while others, including rodents, insects, and weedy plants, have been carried to the islands accidentally.

The good news is that 95% of the archipelago's native species remain intact today, due in large part to the islands' remoteness and relatively recent discovery and settlement by humans. However, it is the islands' isolation that makes the native plants and animals so vulnerable to new arrivals. Separated from many of the species on the continent, the native plant and animals species of Galapagos evolved and thrived in a world with little predation or competition.

While introduced species have been known to cause devastation to native flora and fauna throughout the world, and certainly in Galapagos, the threat from exotics in the marine environment is a more recent phenomenon and remains unstudied in Galapagos. The continuing increase in oceanic traffic, including increases in inter-island traffic related to Galapagos tourism, the number of cargo and other ships moving back and forth from the continent, the number of transoceanic and regional vessels using the waters around Galapagos, and the number of private vessels traveling through the islands, greatly increases the threat of hull and anchor transport of potentially invasive marine species. The successful establishment of introduced marine species elsewhere in the world has resulted in the complete restructuring of marine communities.

When Humans Leave, Other Species Thrive

Patrick Burns

Patrick Burns is a writer whose work has appeared in the environmental publication The Population Press. *In the following viewpoint, Burns argues that reducing the population is the best way to preserve the environment. As evidence, he points to areas that humans have been forced to abandon, such as the irradiated area around the Chernobyl nuclear accident in Ukraine or the Korean Demilitarized Zone. In these areas, the absence of humans has resulted in the return of diverse wildlife. Burns argues that radiation, explosives, and contamination are not as dangerous to wildlife as people, which is why he believes that further world population increase will be devastating to the earth's environment.*

As you read, consider the following questions:

1. How big an area around Chernobyl was evacuated?
2. According to Burns, what may be the home of the last Korean tigers on Earth?
3. What has been the result of the exclusion of humans from the Rocky Flats complex and the Rocky Mountain Arsenal for more than 40 years?

Patrick Burns, "Barbed Wire and Biodiversity," *The Population Press*, vol. 12, no. 2, Spring/Summer 2006. Reproduced by permission.

It is a sobering reality that the best protection for the environment is no people.

When talking about the population and environment, it's sometimes tough to explain how a planet already gut-shot with population and pavement may be further harmed by the addition of another 10 million, 100 million, or 1 billion people.

One way to present the impact of population growth on the environment is to go in the other direction: explain what happens when people and livestock are suddenly excluded from an area for many years.

It is a sobering reality that almost no amount of barbed wire, spent fuel rods, PCBs, landmines or live ammo is as dangerous to wild animals as the mere presence of humans.

Contaminated Landscapes

Across the world today we can find landscapes that have—for a variety of unfortunate reasons—been systematically depopulated for decades at a time.

Sometimes this is due to border conflicts or strife, sometimes it is due to military installations, and sometimes it is due to nuclear or chemical contamination. In almost every case, as soon as humans and captive livestock disappear, wildlife rapidly returns.

It is a sobering reality that almost no amount of barbed wire, spent fuel rods, PCBs, landmines or live ammo is as dangerous to wild animals as the mere presence of humans.

Let me be clear: the point is *not* that we need more biohazard areas in the world, but that people—in and of themselves—have a clear, and almost always negative, impact on wild places and wildlife.

With a world population of 6.5 billion today, and the addition of 3 billion more people expected over the course of

---

After Chernobyl, Wildlife Dies, Then Adapts

[In the immediate aftermath of the Chernobyl nuclear accident] four square kilometres of pine forest in the immediate vicinity of the reactor went ginger brown and died.

Mice embryos simply dissolved, while horses left on an island 6km from the power plant died when their thyroid glands disintegrated.

Cattle on the same island were stunted due to thyroid damage, but the next generation were found to be surprisingly normal.

Now it's typical for animals to be radioactive—too radioactive for humans to eat safely—but otherwise healthy.

Stephen Mulvey, "Wildlife Defies Chernobyl Radiation,"
BBC News, April 20, 2006. http://news.bbc.co.uk.

---

the next 50 years, the bio-hazard of human population growth can only be expected to grow in the years ahead. If you care about wild places and wildlife, you cannot afford to ignore the speed of world population growth.

Chernobyl

Prior to 1986, the area surrounding Chernobyl, Ukraine was an agricultural area populated by about 135,000 people. After an uncontained nuclear power plant accident, however, livestock and crops across a vast area were systematically destroyed, and all of the people within a 2,800 mile area around the Chernobyl plant were evacuated. With the removal of humans from the Chernobyl area has come the return of some of Europe's most endangered species, including lynx, wolves, cranes, beaver, eagles, hawks, wild boar, roe deer, badger, and otters. Populations of human-dependent animals, such as rats, house mice, sparrows and pigeons, have declined. While some folks may imagine that the Chernobyl site must be filled with two-headed frogs, radioactive fish, and sterile deer, scientists have found relatively few visible wildlife side effects. Dr. Ron Chesser, a senior research scientist and genetics professor at the University of Georgia's Savannah River Ecology Laboratory (SREL) in Aiken, South Carolina, notes that "There are no monsters. The Chernobyl zone is actually a very beautiful place with thriving wildlife communities. Without a Geiger-counter, you wouldn't know you were in a highly contaminated place."

Today the 586-square mile [Hanford Nuclear Reservation] site is one of the most contaminated spots on Earth due to nuclear waste, but it also contains the best undisturbed "shrub-steppe" habitat in the Columbia River basin. . . .

The Korean Demilitarized Zone (DMZ)

The Korean Demilitarized Zone is about 2.5 miles wide and 155 miles long, stretching across the entire length of the Korean Peninsula and making it one of the largest unmanned areas in northeast Asia. [It is] festooned with barbed wire, landmines, tank traps, sensors, automatic artillery, and patrolled by scores of thousands of soldiers with "shoot-to-kill" orders. The Korean DMZ is also home to hawks, eagles, antelope, two kinds of rare cranes, frogs, black bears, and roe deer. The DMZ is also rumored to be home to the last Korean tigers on Earth. In total, more than 20,000 migratory fowl utilize the DMZ border area, which encompasses a broad cross-section of Korean ecosystems and landscapes. Some environmentalists fear that a reunification of the two Koreas might spell doom for this vibrant ecosystem, and are urging that steps be taken now to reduce the impact of future roads, bridges and train corridors that might link the two countries.

U.S. Military Weapons Production Facilities

Military weapons production facilities have resulted in the creation of large "no man" zones within the U.S. In Washington State, for example, the Hanford Nuclear Reservation was created as part of the WWII-era Manhattan Project. Today the 586-square mile site is one of the most contaminated spots on Earth due to nuclear waste, but it also contains the best undisturbed "shrub-steppe" habitat in the Columbia River basin, and the only un-dammed stretch of the Columbia River. The healthiest populations of wild Chinook salmon on the river system can be found along the Hanford Reach, and more than 200 species of birds and more than 40 rare plants and animals, such as the long-billed curlew, call it home.

Nuclear Weapons and Research Areas

In Colorado, the Rocky Flats nuclear weapons facility and the Rocky Mountain Arsenal (which produced and stored vast quantities of chemical weapons) systematically kept out humans for more than 40 years. As a result, the 10-square mile Rocky Flats complex has been described as "a rare biological treasure"—one of the last remaining Front Range open spaces with natural prairie grassland—while the Rocky Mountain Arsenal has thriving colonies of prairie dogs and over 100 overwintering bald eagles, as well as trophy-sized mule deer and impressive populations of ferruginous hawks, burrowing owls and mountain plovers.

In Georgia, a 300-square-mile property along the Savannah River was set aside for nuclear research and development more than 50 years ago. For most of the Cold War this site produced plutonium and tritium for atomic bombs. While a small part of the complex remains heavily contaminated, most of the area was left in pristine condition as a security buffer zone—an area that today is home to more than 240 species of birds, 100 species of reptiles and amphibians, and nearly 100 species of freshwater fish. Because Savannah River wildlife was left alone to mature, many state record holders have been caught or trapped here, including the largest South Carolina alligator ever caught (13 feet) and the largest South Carolina largemouth bass. Despite jokes about "glowing frogs," University of Georgia's Whit Gibbons says there is no evidence to date of genetic damage to wildlife. "It's a pretty simple formula," he notes, "The best protection for the environment is no people."

Periodical Bibliography

Ben Blanchard
"Population Growth Threatens East Asian Coasts," *The Religious Consultation*, November 16, 2006. www.religiousconsultation.org.

Alan Caruba
"Global Warming Scares Heat Up," *Capitalism Magazine*, October 5, 2006. www.capmag.com.

Victor Tan Chen
"Global Poverty vs. Global Warming?" *InTheFray*, July 8, 2006. http://inthefray.org.

Mark Clayton
"Is Water Becoming 'The New Oil'?" *Christian Science Monitor Online*, May 28, 2008. www.csmonitor.com.

Steve Connor
"Nature Thrives in Chernobyl," *Ran Prieur*, June 6, 2001. www.ranprieur.com.

Cornelia Dean
"Study Sees 'Global Collapse' of Fish Species," *New York Times*, November 3, 2006.

Daniel Engbar
"Global Swarming," *Slate*, September 10, 2007. www.slate.com.

Lourdes Garcia-Navarro
"Galapagos Plants, Wildlife Under Threat," NPR, August 8, 2005. www.npr.org.

Leiwen Jiang, Malea Hoepf Young, and Karen Hardee
"Population, Urbanization, and the Environment: Growing Cities Stress Their Natural Surroundings, but They Can Also Help Protect Them," *World Watch*, September 1, 2008.

Sean Phillips
"The Water Crisis," *Cosmos*, June 2006.

Matthew Power
"Peter Gleick: Deal With the Water Crisis Now," *Wired*, September 22, 2008. www.wired.com.

Pippa Wysong
"Sugars and Bacterial Growth Kill Off Coral Reefs," *Access Excellence*, October 8, 2006. www.accessexcellence.org.

Population Growth and Economic Development

India Must Give Its Poor Access to Credit to Reduce Population Growth

Atanu Dey

Atanu Dey is an economist at Netcore Solutions in Mumbai, India. In the following viewpoint, Dey argues that poor people have many rational economic reasons for having many children: they need children to care for them in their old age, they need labor to gather water and produce food, and they need to guard against the possibility that some of their children will die young. Unfortunately, Dey argues, what is rational for individuals is disastrous for society as a whole, since overpopulation on a countrywide level can exacerbate poverty. Dey believes that the solution is to provide the poor with credit. For example, he says, this would allow investment in health care, thus reducing the need for more children to insure against the death of their siblings. Dey also argues that female education and other efforts to empower women would help to break the cycle of poverty and population growth.

As you read, consider the following questions:

1. According to Dey, population and poverty are connected to what third factor?

2. What examples does Dey give of institutions that provide social capital?

Atanu Dey, "The Population-Poverty Trap," Atanu Dey on India's Development, June 22, 2004. www.deeshaa.org. Reproduced by permission.

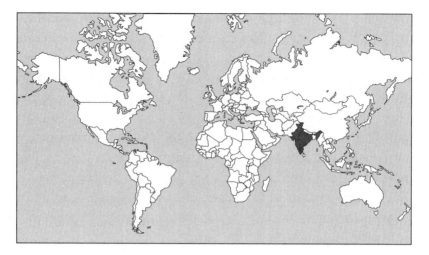

3. According to Dey, why do people have an instinctive desire to procreate?

The causal connection between population and poverty is widely researched and understood by many economists and demographers quite well. There is a causal link between poverty and population, which is mediated by a third component, which is broadly labeled the local resource base. Poverty cannot be understood without reference to the resource base that the population has access to. The three components of population, resources, and poverty are interrelated and influence each other in complex ways that vary across time and space. How these factors influence each other without any of them being the prior cause of the others is as interesting a study as it is depressing to note that the complex interrelations make problems arising within an economy nearly intractable to simple solutions.

Complex systems are often characterized by multiple equilibria. For instance, low population numbers and low population growth rates with high per capita incomes and high educational attainments and low levels of environmental degradation and access to a large resource base could be an equilibrium for an economy. Conversely, another equilibrium for the same economy could be high population numbers with high population growth rates will low per capita incomes and low educational attainments and high levels of environmental degradation and access to a very limited resource base. An economy could be trapped in the latter low level equilibrium and there are no simple ways of nudging the economy out of this trap without multiple interventions applied simultaneously which have their own complex interactions that may be poorly understood. India is caught in the low-level equilibrium characterized above and the challenge is to figure out whether it is possible to transition to a high-level equilibrium and if so how it can be done.

The Poor Make Rational Decisions

For analytical purposes, it is instructive to state the problem of a low-level equilibrium trap at the level of a household. Imagine a low-income household living at a subsistence level in what is called a developing economy. Given its situation in a poor economy, it does not have access to, or is unable to pay for, services that are normally available in developed economies. For instance, the household may not have sufficient income to send its children to school because the children have to supply labor to the household even if schooling were available for free (which it is most often not available at all, free or otherwise.) Further, since children do add to household income and become net assets to the household at an early age in a subsistence economy, there is an incentive to have more children than is socially beneficial leading to a collective action disaster. For the household with a large number of children with low educational attainment, the future is bleak as the competition for resources intensifies and the succeeding generations continue to be trapped in a rapacious vicious cycle of large family sizes and grinding dehumanizing poverty.

Now imagine a moderate-income household in a developed economy. The number of children dictated by the circumstances is low enough for the family to afford to send them to school and thus ensure that succeeding generations will be well placed to continually increase their economic well-being. Given the household decision and the ability to educate its children, collectively the society ensures its future with low population growth rates, high per capita incomes, and so on.

Since children do add to household income and become net assets to the household at an early age in a subsistence economy, there is an incentive to have more children than is socially beneficial.

The essential distinction between the two households above is the environment within which each makes rational utility maximizing decisions. The household in a developed economy has access to capital: its own private capital in terms of its wealth and its income, and the social capital in terms of institutions both private and public such as schools, hospitals, transportation systems, government support, access to credit and so on. In contrast to that, the poor household in a poor country has severe constraints in terms of credit, income, wealth, healthcare, and a million other things. The poor make choices that are "rational" within the constraints they find themselves in and it is unfortunate that their constrained rationality leads to a collective failure that ends up trapping them into an even more constrained situation. In other words, the "environment" is poor for a poor household in a poor country.

Children Economically Benefit the Poor

An example of such a constrained rational response is the number of children that the poor have. The poor, like the rich, have a natural inbuilt instinctive desire to procreate. Having children is an end in itself. Any society that lacks the

Television Improves Women's Status in Rural India

The introduction of cable television improves the status of women: women report lower acceptability of spousal abuse, lower son preference, more autonomy and lower fertility. In addition, cable is associated with increases in school enrollment, perhaps itself an indicator of increased women's status and decision-making authority within the household. . . .

There are several mechanisms through which cable television may affect women's status. For example, television may affect fertility by providing information on family planning services or changing the value of women's time. . . . However, one plausible mechanism is that television exposes rural households to urban lifestyles, values and behaviors that are radically different than their own and that households begin to adopt or emulate some of these. . . .

The possibility that changes in norms, values or attitudes lay behind [study] results is particularly intriguing as a contrast to typically proposed approaches to improving education and women's status or reducing fertility. For example, for education, the emphasis is often on reducing poverty, cutting school fees, building schools and improving school and teacher quality. For fertility, the emphasis is often on factors such as expanding access to family planning goods and services. And efforts to promote women's status are often vague, such as calls to "empower women." In many of these cases, the solutions (such as reducing poverty) are as difficult, to accomplish as the problems they are attempting to solve. . . .

Robert Jensen and Emily Oster,
The Power of TV: Cable Television and Women's Status in India,
September 23, 2008.

genes which predisposes people to children is unlikely to leave very many descendants. But for the poor, the need for children transcends the need for children as an end in themselves. To them, children are productive assets. Where capital is relatively scarce, human labor is the substitute. Labor is required for gathering water, fuel, food production, caring for livestock and other household needs. Children provide that labor required.

Another compulsion that the poor face is the need to have children for old-age security. Lacking any publicly funded social security net, poor people over-insure in terms of having more children than is socially optimal. There are other reasons such as social norms (imitative behavior, for instance), religious (sons are valued for performing the last rites), etc. which compel people to have children. What is rational, or constrained rational, at the household level could on the aggregate translate into a collective failure at the social level. The more children people have in a subsistence economy the more likely they will be to continue to be trapped into a cycle of declining resource availability due to positive feedback effects. In other words, poverty increases the individual incentives for having more children, which in turn reduces the per capita availability of resources both natural and manmade, which leads to deepening of poverty.

Empowerment of women is a factor that is strongly correlated with development. For that to happen, female education is a necessary condition.

Credit Can Break the Cycle

Is there a way out of this cycle of increasing poverty and population growth? I have argued elsewhere that the single most important and binding constraint in this situation is the credit constraint. Given access to credit, a poor household would be able to invest in factors that systematically reduce the need for having a large number of children and also educate the children that they have adequately. If a household could pay for health care, for instance, childhood mortality rates would be low and hence the need to over-insure against childhood death would be mitigated. Having access to credit would also allow families to invest in education and the returns on education could be higher than the cost of education. Higher educational attainment would imply higher household incomes and thus lower incentives to have more children in the next generation. Higher household incomes would on the aggregate translate to greater availability of social security and thus a lower need for children for old-age insurance.

However necessary releasing the credit constraint is, it is clearly not sufficient. There are other factors that need to be simultaneously addressed. For example, empowerment of women is a factor that is strongly correlated with development. For that to happen, female education is a necessary condition.

Canada Should Tie Foreign Aid to Reduction in Population Growth

Tim Murray

Tim Murray is a Canadian writer focusing on environmental issues. In the following viewpoint, he argues that billions of dollars in Canadian aid to places like Zimbabwe and Afghanistan has done little to improve people's lives. Murray argues that much of the aid is being eaten up by population growth, which exacerbates poverty and environmental degradation, and can even undermine democracy. Murray believes that Canada should increase its aid budget, but should refuse to give that aid to countries like Kenya, Haiti, and Ethiopia unless those nations reduce their population growth rates.

As you read, consider the following questions:

1. Robert Mugabe confiscated farms and distributed them to relatives and supporters in which nation?
2. According to Murray, how much more did CIDA (Canadian International Development Agency) spend than its peers to distribute the same amount of aid?
3. According to Murray, what is the Total Fertility Rate (TFR) of Ethiopia?

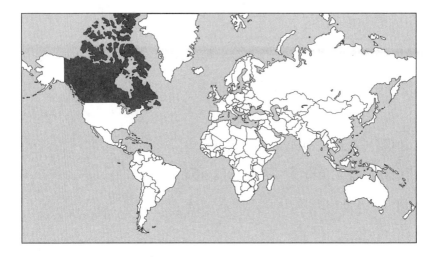

You know the type. The woman who writes love letters to convicts on death row or to men of habitually vicious criminality. The neighbourhood cat lady who the SPCA [Society for the Prevention of Cruelty to Animals] finds in a house of 19 cats coated with feces and filth because she can't turn a stray away. The dog-lover who always selects the lame dog at the animal shelter when corrigible, healthy dogs are available. Such is the lame dog syndrome, and in the field of foreign aid, Canada is a chronic patsy.

Foreign commentator Harry Valentine observed that "Elected Canadian leaders believe that Canadian foreign aid buys Canadian government influence at high government levels in developing nations. Despite receiving Canadian foreign aid, Zimbabwe's Robert Mugabe told nations like Canada to 'mind your business' very bluntly and very directly, in matters pertaining to his genocidal policy of confiscating farms and handing them over to his relatives and supporters. Other African leaders have at least been more diplomatic when essentially saying the same thing. Yet the Canadian government chooses to increase its foreign aid commitment. . . ."

Canada supplied Julius Nyerere with foreign aid during a famine while Lake Tanzania was full of fresh water, while our

Prime Minister toasted him as "Mwalimu" or "Wise Man". Malawi was also rewarded with aid for denying farmers the choice of which crops to grow, while Lake Malawi, comprising 30% of the country, was full of water during that country's famine.

It is no wonder that a Canadian Senate report in 2007 found that $575 billion spent on African development aid has left the continent in worse shape than it was when the aid was first dispensed forty years ago. It revealed that the Canadian International Development Agency (CIDA) spent $12.4 billion since 1968 to sub-Saharan Africa with little in the way of demonstrable results. What former planning minister Ramazan Bashandost said of Canada's most favoured beneficiary, Afghanistan, is most probably true of the scores and scores of countries our taxpayers have sent our earnings to. He remarked that the billions or dollars Afghanistan has received from donor countries has not resulted in "the least improvement" in the lives of Afghani people.

$575 billion spent on African development aid has left the continent in worse shape than it was when aid was first dispensed forty years ago.

It is clear that Canadian foreign aid has not been working. Why? Several answers have been offered. The former Liberal government vowed to deliver "smarter and better aid", focusing on basic, health issues like AIDS, developing the private sector, environmental sustainability. There was a wide consensus that Canadian aid was scattergun and that fewer countries should be favoured with more assistance, half of them African. CIDA itself was too centralized and bureaucratic, spending 15% more than its peer to distribute each dollar of aid. The Opposition critic Keith Martin, a doctor who worked in the region, said that "billions are poured into CIDA and only a trickle of it is seen on the ground."

Yet, despite the waste and the corruption, the clarion call is to spend even more than the $4 billion Ottawa currently spends. In fact, the [Stephen] Harper government intends to double its African aid from 2004 to $2.1 billion next year [2009]. It is thought disgraceful that an affluent country spends more on the military than on foreign aid, particularly when "phantom aid" accounts for over half of that spending in Canada. During last year's famine in Niger, for example, 90% of the food money given by Canada had to be spent on food from Canada. Canada signed on to a UN [United Nations] mandate to have overseas aid reach 0.7% of Gross National Income (GNI), yet still spends well below that. What kind of humanitarianism is this?

But the volume of aid cannot be the measure of its effectiveness. Surely it must be both generous and effective. What is striking about Canadian aid reform proposals are their stunning omission: Family planning. The Martin Liberals spoke of "Health" in terms of lacking AIDS. But death prevention without birth prevention as we have seen so many times is a recipe for disaster and misery on a grander scale. They also spoke of "environmental sustainability". How can an environment be sustainable without population stability? The Harper Conservatives now talk of rewarding those countries that pursue "clean government and democratic values". A good step, but runaway population growth will undermine even sound government. What does Harper reward? In 2007 he flew to Port Au Prince and rewarded the Haitian government with $353 million in CIDA aid for presiding over a nation with a Total Fertility Rate [TFR] of 4.94 and a population growth rate of 2.5% per annum. Haiti becomes Canada's second most favoured aid recipient for having no handle on growth that will negate all the benefits of the aid package.

And who are among Canada's new, narrowed list of favoured "development partners"? Ghana (TFR 3.89), Tanza-

Foreign Aid, in Dollars and U.S. Percentage of Gross National Income, 2004

The U.S. spent more in aid than any other country. As a percentage of its income, though, U.S. aid was smaller than most countries on the list, including Canada.

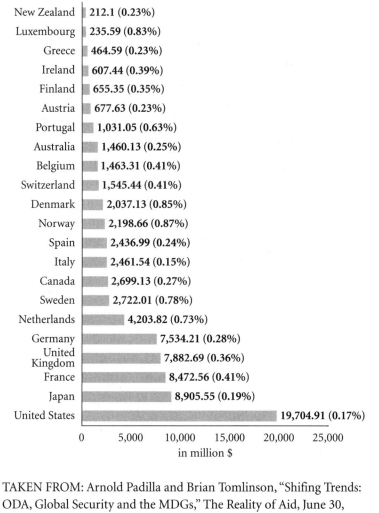

New Zealand	212.1 (0.23%)
Luxembourg	235.59 (0.83%)
Greece	464.59 (0.23%)
Ireland	607.44 (0.39%)
Finland	655.35 (0.35%)
Austria	677.63 (0.23%)
Portugal	1,031.05 (0.63%)
Australia	1,460.13 (0.25%)
Belgium	1,463.31 (0.41%)
Switzerland	1,545.44 (0.41%)
Denmark	2,037.13 (0.85%)
Norway	2,198.66 (0.87%)
Spain	2,436.99 (0.24%)
Italy	2,461.54 (0.15%)
Canada	2,699.13 (0.27%)
Sweden	2,722.01 (0.78%)
Netherlands	4,203.82 (0.73%)
Germany	7,534.21 (0.28%)
United Kingdom	7,882.69 (0.36%)
France	8,472.56 (0.41%)
Japan	8,905.55 (0.19%)
United States	19,704.91 (0.17%)

0   5,000   10,000   15,000   20,000   25,000
in million $

TAKEN FROM: Arnold Padilla and Brian Tomlinson, "Shifing Trends: ODA, Global Security and the MDGs," The Reality of Aid, June 30, 2006. http://www.realityofaid.org.

nia (TFR 4.77), Mozambique (TFR 5.29). And Ethiopia (TFR 5.1) and Kenya (TFR 4.82) are cited by Canada now as "good performers".

It is my considered opinion that these "good performers" are more like lame dogs. My question is this—would you give money to an alcoholic panhandler, or would you tell him to go home and clean up his act?

Haiti becomes Canada's second most favoured aid recipient for having no handle on growth that will negate all the benefits of the aid package.

I rather think that Haiti, Ethiopia, Kenya, et al. should be told to take a hike. Then again, it seems that is about all they have been doing anyway.

My prescription? Increase foreign aid dramatically, but make it strictly conditional on compliance with our birth control guidelines. If Mr. Mugabe tells us to mind our own business, then let's do that. And we'll mind our money as well.

It's like this, Oh Wise Mwalimu: No condoms, no food. Get it?

Western Europe Needs More Immigration to Fuel Population and Economic Growth

The Economist

The Economist *is a British magazine that specializes in international and business news. In the following viewpoint, the editors note that anti-immigration sentiment in European nations has been rising. They attribute this rise to an influx of immigrants from poor countries, especially from new members of the European Union like Romania and Bulgaria. The editors argue that this flow of immigrants will slow soon since there are labor shortages in eastern Europe and wages there are rising. But the editors also warn that slowing population growth in western Europe will cause labor shortages there unless immigrants take up the slack. They suggest that western European governments should be encouraging immigration, not discouraging it.*

As you read, consider the following questions:

1. According to *The Economist* editors, which immigrants in Italy face popular prejudice?

2. According to polls, which European nation has the most positive attitude towards migration?

3. According to *The Economist* editors, Europe's native-born workforce will shrink by how much by the middle of the century?

The Economist, "The Trouble with Migrants," Economist.com, November 22, 2007. Republished with permission of *The Economist*, conveyed through Copyright Clearance Center, Inc.

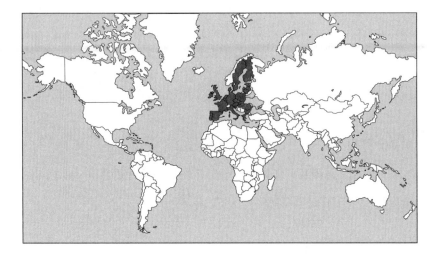

Cast your eye around Europe, and you find a funk about foreigners. Denmark's voters have given the anti-immigration Danish People's Party its fourth successive rise in voting share. The Swiss gave 29% of their votes to the xenophobic Swiss People's Party. An anti-foreigner party is the second biggest in Norway. A fifth of Flemish voters in Belgium back the far-right Vlaams Belang.

In France, Nicolas Sarkozy won the presidency in May after aping the anti-immigrant rhetoric of the National Front's Jean-Marie Le Pen. He now talks of inculcating French values. Next year, when France has the European Union presidency, he will promote a similar idea at EU level. His new ministry of national identity and immigration has proposed quotas on immigrants from some regions that may be a ploy to keep out the dark-skinned. He has passed a law to limit immigration for family unification, which allows DNA testing to prove genetic ties.

French policy is measured by comparison with recent actions in Italy. After a Romanian migrant killed an Italian woman in Rome, Romano Prodi's government approved a decree to make it easier to expel EU citizens who are deemed a threat to public security. This pandered to the popular prejudice that Italy's half a million Romanian immigrants, often Roma (gypsies), are more criminal than other new arrivals. But it achieved little. Vigilantes attacked Romanians; police destroyed Roma camps. But as of mid-November, only 117 people had been served with expulsion orders; far fewer had actually gone.

Why are Europe's voters and politicians so stirred up? The short answer is that rates of immigration, from inside and outside the EU are high, and have been rising for years. A report by Goldman Sachs, an investment bank, suggests that since 2001 migration has added 0.5% a year to Europe's workforce. It concludes that immigration in Europe has outstripped even inflows to America. In many European countries the stock of the foreign-born population has never been higher. As much as 24% of the Swiss population was born elsewhere, as was 12% of Belgium's.

The numbers alone do not explain why some countries are anxious and others less so. France and Denmark have foreign-born shares of the population of only 8% and 6.5% respectively. Some countries that are relatively more relaxed about immigration have much bigger shares: Sweden has 12% and Ireland 11%, for example. One explanation is that an inrush of immigrants may not provoke a backlash so long as the economy is strong.

Rates of immigration from inside and outside the EU are high, and have been rising for years.

Worries about immigration from poor countries have been around for years. The fresh element in many west European countries is a concern about immigration from new EU members in eastern Europe. Since the accession of eight countries from the region in 2004, followed by Romania and Bulgaria in January 2007, large numbers of migrant workers have moved (often legally and temporarily) from east to west. Britain, Swe-

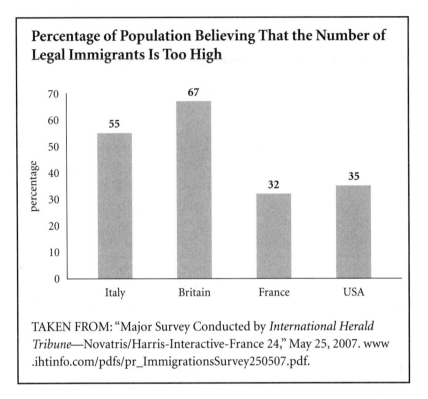

Percentage of Population Believing That the Number of Legal Immigrants Is Too High

TAKEN FROM: "Major Survey Conducted by *International Herald Tribune*—Novatris/Harris-Interactive-France 24," May 25, 2007. www .ihtinfo.com/pdfs/pr_ImmigrationsSurvey250507.pdf.

den and Ireland opened up fully to workers from the east in May 2004 and have taken in many highly educated migrants, helping to sustain their long economic upswings. Countries that have seen housing booms have imported hundreds of thousands of lower-skilled workers, often from the east.

Spain alone is thought by the European Commission to be home to some 547,000 adults of working age from Romania and Bulgaria. Yet Spaniards, according to a poll this month for France 24, a television station, appear untroubled. They have the sunniest attitudes of all Europeans towards migration, with 43% of respondents saying that immigrants are a boon to Europe and 55% believing that they are good for the economy. The same poll suggested that 42% of Britons think immigrants are good for the economy, although fewer believe they benefit the country overall.

Yet even in Britain there is creeping anxiety about high immigration from within the EU. This is partly to do with foreign nationals (all those skilled Poles in London) who now take roughly half of all the new jobs being created in Britain. Other gripes are that schools, hospitals and roads are getting overcrowded. After its experience since 2004, Britain decided last January to keep its doors shut to migrant workers from Romania and Bulgaria. Gordon Brown, the prime minister, aware of Mr. Sarkozy's electoral success, even talked at the Labour Party conference of "British jobs for British workers". He has pledged to restrict immigrants from any countries that join the EU in future.

For all the current fretting about too many foreigners, a chronic shortage of suitable workers may be felt most acutely in the countries that seem most hostile to outsiders.

Such talk may please voters, but the ebb and flow of EU migrants seems likely to be driven more by economics than by politicians. In the short run the rate of migration within the EU is likely to slow. Demand for foreign labour in western Europe may drop as housing markets slow and construction falls off. Years of strong growth in the east, combined with a steady outflow of workers, have led to serious labour shortages that are driving up wages. That reduces the incentive to leave, and increases the incentive to return.

In truth the bad demographic outlook of much of western and eastern Europe will make the continent increasingly reliant on foreign labour. And one irony is that, for all the current fretting about too many foreigners, a chronic shortage of suitable workers may be felt most acutely in the countries that seem most hostile to outsiders. Germany has kept its labour markets closed to new EU members until 2011, but it now admits to a skills shortage. This month it eased the restrictions on migrant workers in the mechanical and electrical-engineering industries.

Immigration already accounts for most of the limited population growth in Europe. Ageing populations, combined with the natives' lack of ability, or inclination, to do many jobs, mean that more foreign workers are likely to be needed. By one estimate Europe's native-born workforce will shrink by 44m by the middle of the century. Skilled workers will be in especially short supply. Those calling most fiercely for foreigners to go home may come to regret what they wished for.

Japan's Population Decline May Help Its Economic Growth

William Pesek

William Pesek is a columnist for Bloomberg News. In the following viewpoint, Pesek points out that economists usually believe that shrinking populations slow productivity and hurt the economy. However, Pesek reports, a Hong Kong economist named Sharmila Whelan has argued that Japan's shrinking population may actually improve Japan's economy. Whelan points out that countries like Sudan have rapidly growing populations but stagnant economies. Whelan believes that the cultural and social changes caused by the aging population will force the Japanese to innovate, and that this will increase productivity. Pesek, however, is not sure that the Japanese will actually reinvent their economy as Whelan thinks they will.

As you read, consider the following questions:

1. According to a government report, who must Japanese companies hire if the workforce is not to shrink by a third?

2. According to Whelan, was the Dutch Republic in the fourteenth century hurt by demographic trends similar to those of modern day Japan?

William Pesek, "Viewpoint: Defying Japanese Demographics," *International Herald Tribune*, December 7, 2006. www.iht.com. Reprinted with permission.

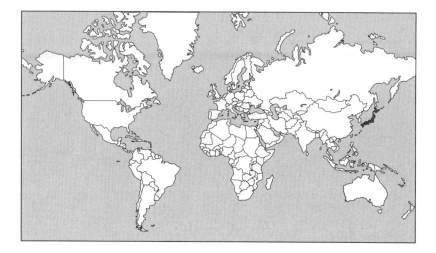

3. Is Japanese productivity high or low compared to the other Group of Seven industrialized economies?

Here is a worthy question for the *Freakonomics* guys: is a shrinking population, contrary to conventional wisdom, actually good for an economy?

Last year [2005], Steven Levitt, an economist at the University of Chicago, and a writer, Stephen Dubner, made a splash with *Freakonomics*, a book that turns traditional economics upside down by puzzling out everyday conundrums. The global demographic quirks would seem a perfect candidate for their attention.

Most economists will roll their eyes at the question itself.

[An] economist committed demographic heresy by arguing that fewer people will brighten the Japanese outlook.

Well of course, they will argue, dwindling ranks will lead to less growth. Shrinking populations reduce labor forces, crimp productivity, hurt tax receipts and raise debt levels.

At least in the case of Japan, Sharmila Whelan of CLSA Asia-Pacific Markets in Hong Kong begs to differ. In a September report, the economist committed demographic heresy by arguing that fewer people will brighten the Japanese outlook.

The plot has thickened since Whelan's report began making the rounds. Last month, the government said that in 2005, the population shrank for the first time—excluding a dip during World War II—since Japan began compiling data in 1899. The birthrate fell to a record 1.25 babies per woman, well below the 2.1 needed to maintain the current population of 127 million.

Complicating things, a rapidly aging population means Japanese demographics are becoming ever more lopsided. A recent government report said the Japanese workforce would likely shrink by as much as a third by 2050 if more women and elderly workers are not hired.

An aversion to immigration does not help. While estimates vary too widely to bother mentioning here, Japan may need to import millions of workers in the years ahead to fill gaps in the labor pool. Never mind that those of us living in ultra-crowded Japan wonder where we will fit several million more bodies—the economy needs the manpower.

If economic potential were only about cheap labor, money would be rushing to Sudan and Myanmar

---

Some observers are finding silver linings. In a new book, *The Japanese Money Tree*, an economist, Andrew Shipley, takes an intriguing look at the bright side of a graying Japan.

"Investors are ignoring an arguably much more important demographic shift," Shipley wrote. "A younger generation of politicians, executives and policy makers is poised to take charge."

Whelan said fewer people would do for Japan what the previous and current Japanese prime ministers, Junichiro Koizumi and Shinzo Abe, have been unable to do: catalyze an innovation boom that could make Japan more productive.

"High population growth alone never delivered high economic growth," Whelan wrote. "If it did, this report would be about Africa, not Japan."

It is a good point. When you ask executives why they are investing in China, two words come up immediately: cheap labor.

Yet if economic potential were only about cheap labor, money would be rushing to Sudan and Myanmar.

In the same way, if population growth were all that mattered, then Indonesia, the Philippines and Cambodia would be thriving.

Whelan's optimism is based in part on history. Economic growth, she argues, tends to be driven by "specialization, innovation and trade." Investment, like labor, tends to go where returns are highest. As Japan moves more toward a knowledge-based economy driven by increased research and development, its citizens will prosper.

Similar demographic trends did not hold back the Venetian economy in the 11th century, Whelan said. Nor did it imperil the Dutch Republic in the 14th century. Likewise, Whelan said, "in the coming decade, Japan's shrinking population is the least of her problems as far as growth goes."

The real challenge is letting the forces of creative destruction championed by the economist Joseph Schumpeter shake up the rigid Japanese system. Schumpeter argued that entrepreneurial innovation creates economic growth and can overturn a corporate giant, as Apple and Microsoft did to IBM.

It is already happening, Whelan said, pointing to renewed foreign interest in Japan, a rise in mergers and acquisitions and a growing number of start-up companies. To her, it all adds up to a more dynamic and flexible corporate sector.

Yet the key now is accelerating efforts to make Japan Inc. more efficient. That is much easier said than done. Japanese

South Korea's Falling Fertility Rate

Like Japan and other nations, South Korea has experienced a declining fertility rate. The graph shows that in 1970, South Korean women had an average of 4.5 children; today that number is 1.26.

Total fertility rate, %

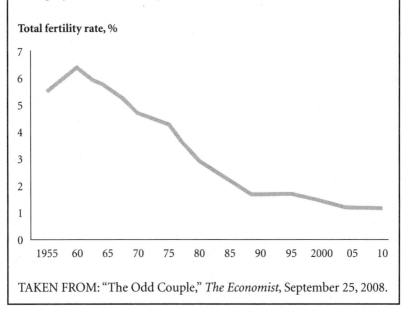

TAKEN FROM: "The Odd Couple," *The Economist*, September 25, 2008.

people work some of the longest hours among developed countries and yet worker productivity tends to be the lowest among the Group of Seven industrialized economies.

Far from being alarmed by the dearth of options, [economist Sharmila] Whelan contends that, pushed against a demographic wall, Japan will reinvent itself.

Increasing innovation and productivity is the only way that high-cost Japan can maintain its living standard amid the rise of low-cost China, India and Southeast Asia. Doubts that the Japanese government is sufficiently focused on raising productivity—ones that I share—put Whelan in contrarian territory.

In a recent book, *Shrinking Population Economics: Lessons from Japan*, a former Japanese Ministry of Finance official, Akihiko Matsutani, argued that the shrinking population of Japan would steadily reduce growth. From 2009 to 2020, Matsutani predicted gross domestic product would fall 1.1 percent a year.

Fresh thinking is needed since the Japanese fiscal situation limits throwing money at the problem as an option. The Organization for Economic Cooperation and Development puts the Japanese public debt at 170 percent of gross domestic product, the most among industrialized economies.

Far from being alarmed by the dearth of options, Whelan contends that, pushed against a demographic wall, Japan will reinvent itself.

"Access to labor, technology and capital are the least of Japan's problems," Whelan said. "Creating an environment where there is unhindered entry and exit of new businesses and new ideas are born resulting in continuous innovation and cost savings is the greater challenge. Japan has a long way to go, but the process has started."

Let us hope so. Otherwise, the world's No. 2 economy could shrink along with the ranks of the Japanese.

Russia's Economy Is Hurt by Poor Health, Not by Population Decline

Dietwald Claus

Dietwald Claus is a public affairs consultant and a business journalist for the Moscow News. *In the following viewpoint, Claus argues that Russia's declining population is not actually a problem: many nations, he points out, have a lower population density than Russia, and, in any case, nations with a high birth rate do not necessarily experience strong economic growth. Even Russia's low life expectancy might have an upside, he argues, in that a younger population would be less indebted to old Soviet-style economic ideas. The real problem in Russia, Claus suggests, is that Russians are not sufficiently economically productive, in large part because they are unhealthy. Russia, he argues, needs not more babies, but less drinking, less smoking, and better health care and education.*

As you read, consider the following questions:

1. According to Claus, what is Russia's current population density?

2. According to Claus, what is the relationship between population size, population density, and economic performance?

Dietwald Claus, "Myths and Realities of Russia's Population Crisis," Johnson's Russia List, March 22, 2006. www.cdi.org. Reproduced by permission.

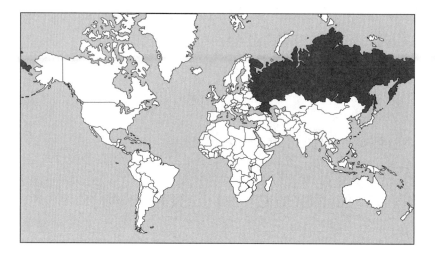

3. According to Claus, what factors are more important in military success than numbers?

While at odds with each other on almost everything else, Russia watchers and Russian officialdom seem to agree on the problem of Russia's demographic decline. That there is a problem is out of the question. Unfortunately, much of the debate about Russia's demography is rubbish. Though I will not claim to have solutions for the real problems, I would like to debunk some obvious myths that seem to permeate a significant part of the public debate on the issue, whether by experts or laypeople.

Decline Is No Disaster

Myth 1) If Russia's population continues to decline, Russia will cease to exist.

That's patent nonsense. Population density has nothing to do with whether a country can exist or not. But, even if there was a lower population density limit at which countries magically disappear, Russia really has not much to worry about. Even the worst case scenario of only 80 million people on Russia's territory by 2075 would still leave Russia with a greater population density than contemporary Canada. Russia's current population density is about 8.5 people per square kilometer, more than three times that of Australia, and twice that of Canada. And last time I checked, Canada's still on the map. It's actually hard to miss there. So, Russia's population has a lot of shrinking to do before Russia is going to disappear, and we can stop worrying about this for the moment.

Even the worst case scenario of only 80 million people on Russia's territory by 2075 would still leave Russia with a greater population density than contemporary Canada.

Myth 2) If Russia's population declines, other[s] will take over its territory.

That's really just a correlate of Myth 1, and equally non-sensical: Yes, much of Russia's territory is pretty empty. But so is that of Canada and Australia, and quite a number of other countries, including the USA. The reason for this is that nobody wants to live there. There is an explanation why much of Siberia was settled by fugitives and convicts—given the choice, people [would] much rather settle where the weather is reasonably warm and the soil fertile. So, folks are not exactly lining up to move into the empty vastness of Russia's East.

Of course, some people seem to believe that if the Russian East is not settled systematically by Russians, China might just forget the place belongs to Russia. Tired of paying for Russian oil, gas, and other resources, it will instead move in and cut out the middleman. This line of reasoning is so absurd in so many ways I will limit myself to a very obvious rebuttal: the Chinese government is highly unlikely to start annexing Russian territory, even if it wanted to, for the very simple reason that Russia has a lot more relative firepower there. Russian nukes are a lot closer to Beijing than Chinese nukes are to Moscow. I leave the rest of this morbid scenario to those with a greater tolerance for absurd apocalyptic visions than I have.

Immigration Is No Disaster

Myth 3) If Russia's population continues to decline, there will be an invasion of immigrants.

That's just stupid. Whether Russia's population is shrinking, expanding, or staying the same makes no difference to people who wants to come and live here. Population size, density, and dynamics have no bearing on immigration; just ask the Dutch, Germans, or Pakistanis.

That being said, there is something absurd about this argument: on the one hand, everybody seems to complain that not enough people live in Russia, but when people try to actually come, live, and work here, it's no good either.

Immigration has traditionally been a major factor in the economic success of nations—just witness the US, Canada, Australia for contemporary examples. Historic examples would be Prussia, whose rise to economic fortune, political power, and cultural prowess had much to do with Frederick II's enlightened immigration policy. Russia, too, has fared quite well in the past when it adopted generous immigration policies. There is no reason in principle to assume it won't do so now.

Everybody seems to complain that not enough people live in Russia, but when people try to actually come, live, and work here, it's not good either.

Does this mean I am in favor of uncontrolled and unlimited immigration? Of course not. I'm not in favor of uncontrolled and unlimited anything. A modern society needs rules, and that includes rules for immigration. What a modern society does not need is tribalism, which brings us to the next point:

Myth 4) If there is an invasion of immigrants, Russia will cease being Russian.

This is outright xenophobic [afraid of foreigners], racist, and stupid: if Russia gave citizenship to all those Chinese, Azeris, and what have you, would Russia cease to be Russian? Only if being a Russian citizen is conditional on being Slavic. But, since when did being a Slav have anything to do with having Russian citizenship? The answer to that is obvious: it never did. Any assertion to the contrary simply displays a complete ignorance of Russia's history, culture, and ethnography.

And even *if* being Slavic was once a prerequisite for being a Russian citizen, would it not be time to stop living with a tribal mindset? All successful civilizations of the past and present have been and are multi-cultural. This is no argument against Russian language and institutions being the unifying element of Russian society—far from it—but it's an argument against tribalism.

Big Population Does Not Equal Good Economy

Myth 5) Russia needs a large population to have a good economy.

Balderdash. Countries like Luxemburg and Switzerland have very small populations, but nobody would argue their economies are anything but stellar. Nigeria has a huge population, its economy, however, isn't doing so well. The USA has a population about ten times that of Canada, but both are doing just fine economically. There is no relationship whatsoever between population size, population density, and economic performance. Any assertion to the contrary is just ignorant.

Myth 6) Russia's shrinking population is bad for the economy.

Nonsense. Changes in the number of people in a country have nothing to do with its economic performance. Let's assume we are having an annual population growth of 10%, and the productivity of every member of the population is equal and does not change, then the economic growth should be 10% as well. 10% economic growth seems like a good thing, but in reality, if it is caused by a 10% population growth, this economic growth really means nothing. Nobody in such a country is better off. All you are having is more people who live no better or worse than before.

Of course, the inverse is equally true. If the population declines by x%, while each member of society remains equally productive, overall GDP [gross domestic products] shrinks by x%, while per capita GDP remains unaffected. In other words, changes in total population are neutral in respect to GDP per capita.

At the risk of offending mothers and romantics everywhere, I'll state it bluntly: children make us poorer.

Not Just Growth, but Growth Per Person

Myth 7) Russia needs to increase its birth rate.

That's actually a really, really dumb idea. Russia needs an increased birth rate as much as it needs more snow. Children may be a biological necessity, but since infants and children are not economically productive members of society, they are bad news for the economy. If a lot of children are born, a lot of economic resources will go into feeding, clothing, housing, and educating them—these expenses are, at least in the short run, an economic net-loss. So, obviously, children do not contribute to the growth of GDP.

In fact, children decrease the productivity of a society. After all, somebody has to look after them—and time spent looking after children is time not spent engaging in economically productive activities. Logically, the more children somebody has, the less economically productive this person will be. Thus, high birth rates also mean decreased general economic productivity, negatively impacting GDP growth.

At the risk of offending mothers and romantics everywhere, I'll state it bluntly: children make us poorer. In order to maintain any given level of GDP per capita, productivity of the working population has to increase at the same rate as the birth rate just to maintain current levels of GDP per capita. Anything less would lead to a decrease in GDP per capita and consequently to a pauperization of the general population.

Birth rates around the replacement level (2.1 children per woman, on average) seem to be economically harmless. Anything much above that, however, leads to trouble. If you don't believe this, just look at the facts: no country with a birth rate significantly above replacement rate is doing well on any scale, whether economically or politically.

Myth 8) Russia needs to grow its GDP.

Wrong. Russia needs to grow its GDP per capita. Economic growth by itself does not mean increased average economic welfare. Economic growth only leads to an increase in overall economic welfare if it is the result of an increased GDP per capita. GDP per capita matters. GDP doesn't. Write that down. Any economic policy not targeted at increasing GDP per capita, preferably through increased productivity, is meaningless.

These aren't exactly new insights, but considering the debates currently taking place about Russia's economy in and outside Russia, the obvious does seem to need repeating.

If Russia's current low life expectancy means that the generation whose ideas about public life are largely informed by Marxism-Leninism is dying off quickly, this means that demand for public policies based on Marxist-Leninist ideas is decreasing.

New Blood

Myth 9) Russia's low life expectancy is a bad thing.

Not necessarily true. Those of you with no stomach for a little cynicism may want to skip this section, the rest, please bear with me.

This point is not about economics per se, but about some larger sociological factors, which also impact on economics.

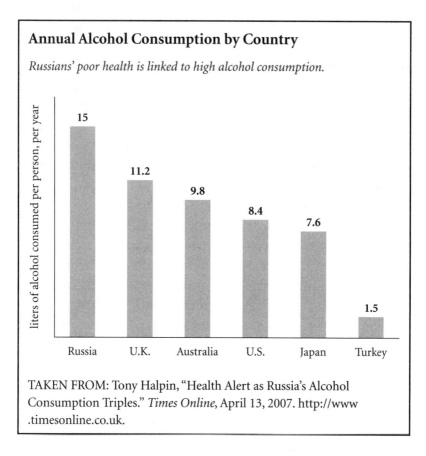

Annual Alcohol Consumption by Country

Russians' poor health is linked to high alcohol consumption.

liters of alcohol consumed per person, per year

- Russia: 15
- U.K.: 11.2
- Australia: 9.8
- U.S.: 8.4
- Japan: 7.6
- Turkey: 1.5

TAKEN FROM: Tony Halpin, "Health Alert as Russia's Alcohol Consumption Triples." *Times Online*, April 13, 2007. http://www.timesonline.co.uk.

There is no adult in Russia today who was not born under the previous regime. In other words, the vast majority of the population has been brought up to think along lines of official Marxist-Leninist ideology about a wide range of things, including public policy in general, and [e]conomics in particular. As time passes, these generations seem to forget all the bad things about the previous regime, and increasingly become rather nostalgic about Soviet economic policies. Since these generations also tend to vote more than younger people who are not overly affected by such ideas, government policies in Russia must by necessity take into considerations the sentiments of the older generations. But since Marxist-Leninist ideas are not exactly a good basis for sound public policy, accommodating ideas based on Marxist-Leninist thinking cannot be good public policy. If Russia's current low life expectancy means that the generation whose ideas about public life are largely informed by Marxism-Leninism is dying off quickly, this means that demand for public policies based on Marxist-Leninist ideas is decreasing. Politically, this can only be a good thing, with definite benefits for the economy.

There, I've said it. Breathe in, breathe out, breathe in. Calm down. This is a 'there's a good side to almost everything' kind of situation, not a *Soylent Green* scenario.

Myth 10) Russia needs a big population because it needs a big army.

This one is so inane, it hurts. If population size was the main factor determining military capacity, China would have taken over Korea, the USA would have beaten the Vietcong, Afghanistan would be part of Russia, Taiwan part of Red China, Canada part of the USA . . . you get the idea. Throughout history, size did not matter much in military affairs. The Greeks were hopelessly outnumbered by the Persians, the dreaded Mongol hordes, contrary to common belief, were actually much fewer in number than most of the armies they defeated, and Frederick II of Prussia was significantly outnumbered in almost all the wars he fought. What matters in military affairs are first and foremost training, equipment, and morale. Numbers do make a difference, but are far less important than most civilians believe.

Russia's armed forces face a lot of problems, no question. Military reforms should focus on training, equipment, and morale—worrying about its size really isn't an issue, at least not from a purely military security point of view.

The Real Issue Is Quality, Not Quantity

Much of the current debate on Russia's demographic situation is nonsense. Russia is not going to disappear from the map because of its shrinking population. It's not going to lose territory to the Chinese, it's not going to be overrun by hostile armies, and it's not going to be taken over by those swarthy immigrants from the South. Neither Russia nor the Russian narod are going the way of the Dodo any time soon.

Now that we have dealt with the nonsense, let's take a brief look at the real issue:

[The issue is] not Russia's overall population is too small or shrinking too much [but that] the share of economically productive people in Russia is too small, and arguably shrinking. Russians smoke more, drink more hard liquor, have more abortions, have more preventable diseases, drive more dangerously, and eat less healthy than most people in other industrialized nations. Sick people are not productive workers. As a result, for each unit of GDP per capita, each Russian worker has to work harder and longer than each Canadian worker, and each Russian unit of money has to be more productive than each Canadian unit of money.

Consequently, it does not matter whether Russia has 100 or 500 million inhabitants: if the proportion and productivity of economically active population does not increase, GDP per capita will not increase, and nobody will be better off. The most important task for Russia's government is to increase the proportion and productivity of its economically active population.

If Russians drank as little as the Swiss, ate as well as the Japanese, drove as carefully as the Dutch, and continued to work as hard as, well, Russians, doubling Russia's GDP per capita in ten years would be a very modest goal.

What Russia needs is not more babies, but more healthy people who are able to work.

Healthier People, Healthier Economy

Too many Russian men drink, smoke, drive, and infect themselves to premature death. Too many Russian women suffer from the health effects of too many abortions, or have too many babies who die too early. Demographically, it does not matter whether people aren't born at all, or whether they die prematurely. Economically, the difference is significant, since bearing and raising children only to have them die early is a waste of resources. A single healthy person with a good education employed in a good job when he reaches maturity is better than two sickly people who line up for government handouts.

Historically, this is how the rich countries became rich: they improved labor productivity by simultaneously reducing birth and mortality rates. Incidentally, these factors also contributed to a significant population growth. But, since this population growth went hand in hand with an even greater increase of the size and productivity of the economically active population, today's rich nations were able to combine rapid population growth with rapid economic development.

What Russia needs is not more babies, but more healthy people who are able to work. For this, it has to find both short- and long-term solutions, including, but not limited to, a significant increase of excise taxes on alcohol and cigarettes, smart immigration policies, public education campaigns on general and reproductive health, more stringent enforcement of traffic and workplace safety rules, and improved medical care. Some of these policies will cost little, while others may prove expensive in the short term.

Clearly, none of this should come as news to any literate person. But, considering the tendency of the current demographic debate in Russia to focus on non-issues such as population size, birth rates, territorial integrity, or military security, it seems necessary to point out the trivial. There have been serious voices suggesting natalist policies [those promoting human reproduction]—it should be clear to anyone that this would be a serious blow against the future of Russia. Any fear mongering regarding the security of Russia's territory or identity due to a decreased overall population should be nipped in the bud, and natalist ideology should be exposed as the idiocy it really is.

Periodical Bibliography

Virginia Abernethy "Optimism and Overpopulation," *The Atlantic Monthly*, December 1994.

Gary Becker "Disease, Population, and Economic Progress," The Becker-Posner Blog, December 27, 2004. www.becker-posner-blog.com.

The Economist "How To Deal with a Falling Population," July 26, 2007.

Paul B. Farrell "Peak oil? Global Warming? No, It's Boomsday!" *MarketWatch*, January 26, 2009. www.marketwatch.com.

Malcolm Gladwell "The Risk Pool," *The New Yorker*, August 28, 2006.

Paul Goble "Window on Eurasia: Economic Crisis Compounds Russia's Demographic Decline," *Window On Eurasia*, October 28, 2008. www.windowoneurasia.blogspot.com.

IRIN "Burkina Faso: Population Growth Outstrips Economic Gains," January 21, 2009. www.irinnews.org.

Philip Longman "The Depopulation Bomb," *Conservation Magazine*, July–September 2006.

Donald Mann "A No-Growth Steady State Economy Must Be Our Goal," *Negative Population Growth*. www.npg.org.

Nuwa Nuwagaba "Only Poverty Reduction Will Curtail Population Growth," *African Health Sciences*, March 2008.

Muhammad Yahya Waliullah "Demographic Dividend: One Too Many," *Dawn Online*, July 20, 2008. www.dawn.com.

Workpermit.com "Canadian Population Growth Driven by Needed Immigration," March 14, 2007. www.workpermit.com.

 GLOBAL VIEWPOINTS

CHAPTER 4

Population Growth and Society

Kenyan Violence Is Propelled by Growth in Young Male Population

Gunnar Heinsohn

Gunnar Heinsohn is a sociologist with the Raphael Lemkin Institute for Comparative Genocide Research at the University of Bremen in Germany. In the following viewpoint, he argues that the explosion of violence in 2007–2008, following disputed elections, was due to shifts in population. Specifically, Heinsohn points out that Kenya's high population growth has meant that a large percentage of the population is composed of young men. Because Kenya has a relatively high standard of living, Heinsohn says, these men have high expectations, but their numbers mean there are few jobs. The large percentage of restless young men ensures violence and unrest, Heinsohn believes.

As you read, consider the following questions:

1. According to Heinsohn, how much did per capita income in Kenya grow between 1975 and 2006?

2. In 2007, how many children on average were born to each Kenyan woman?

3. According to Heinsohn, what years constitute the "fighting age" for males?

Gunnar Heinsohn, "Kenya's Violence: Exploding Population," *International Herald Tribune*, January 17, 2008. www.iht.com. Reprinted with permission.

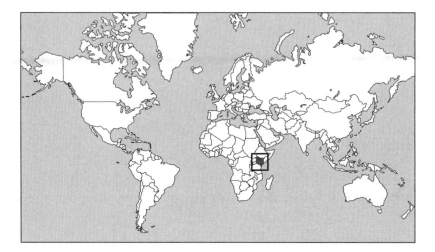

M ost foreign observers of the [2007–2008] violence in Kenya have blamed it on the abuse of power by Kikuyu politicians, a rigged election and economic hardships.

But why now?

Corruption, ethnic rivalry and voting irregularities, after all, are as old as Kenyan independence in 1963.

One reason Kenyans have been able to cope with these troubles heretofore is because they've also been enjoying greater political freedom and prosperity. Between 1975 and 2006, per capita income grew at least threefold. And since 1997, the number of political parties competing in national elections has grown from 11 to 26.

As in so many other African countries, Kenya's exploding violence can be traced to an exploding population that often goes unnoted by local and international media alike.

Violent Demography

No wonder the recent massacres took even Kenyans by surprise. Wangan Maalhai, a Kenyan who was awarded the 2004

Nobel Peace Prize, told an interviewer she was stunned "that it could happen in Kenya"—as if this pearl of East Africa was not to be compared with Congo, Rwanda, Sierra Leone, Somalia, Sudan, Uganda and all the other African countries afflicted by bloodshed and chaos.

But does Kenya really have nothing in common with its violence-plagued neighbors?

As in so many other African countries, Kenya's exploding violence can be traced to an exploding population that often goes unnoted by local and international media alike.

In only 80 years, Kenya's population has jumped from 2.9 million to 37 million. Had America grown at the same rate since 1928, when it had 120 million people, it would now have 1.56 billion citizens.

Kenya belongs to a group of some 40 countries that have extremely high population growth—rates of increase that I call "demographic armament." In a typical nation of this group, every 1,000 males aged 40 to 44 are succeeded by at least 2,500 boys aged 0 to 4. In Kenya there are 4,190 such boys.

By contrast, America meets the criteria of "demographic neutrality," in which 1,000 men aged 40 to 44 are followed by 900 to 1,400 boys aged 0 to 4 (in the United States, the figure is 977 boys). Britain, with just 677 boys between 0 and 4 replacing every 1,000 males 40 to 44, is in the category of "demographic capitulation." Germany, with just 474 boys following every 1,000 men, provides the most prominent example of "demographic suicide" (fewer than 650 boys replacing 1,000 men).

Between 1950 and 1985, Kenya's total fertility rate (children per woman's lifetime) hovered around eight. In 2007, each Kenyan woman still gave birth to an average of 5 children (compared to 2 in the United States and 1.6 in Britain), and

---

Weak Institutions Contributed to the Violence in Kenya

Until late 2007, Kenya was considered one of the most stable countries in Africa. It has functioned as East Africa's financial and communications hub, the headquarters of many international nongovernmental organizations, and a magnet for tourism. Analysts looked favorably upon its healthy and broad-based economic expansion under President Mwai Kibaki, which stood in marked contrast to the growth of countries such as Angola and Equatorial Guinea that depend on the export of a single commodity—oil. Yet disputed elections in late December 2007 spurred outbreaks of violence across the country that killed more than six-hundred people. That prompted some fears that Kenya would split on tribal lines and descend into prolonged unrest. Experts say such a scenario is unlikely, but also suggest that prior depictions of Kenya's stability were premature. Kenya is a young democracy, they say, and its weak institutions—not inherent ethnic divisions—are at the root of the current political crisis.

Stephanie Hanson, "Understanding Kenya's Politics,"
Council on Foreign Relations, January 25, 2008. www.cfr.org.

---

there were 40 newborn babies for every 10 deaths (the corresponding figures for the U.S. is 14 births for every 8 deaths; for Britain, it's 10 for 10).

Youth Bulge

As a result, Kenyan men have a median age of 18 years (compared to 35 in the United States, 39 in Britain), and 42 percent of Kenyan males are under 15 (U.S.: 20 percent, Britain: 17 percent).

And because of higher living standards, these younger Kenyans are much more vital and ambitious than their predecessors.

Thus Kenya provides a textbook example of domestic violence that is driven by what I call a "youth bulge"—a period of rapid demographic growth in which 30 to 40 percent of all males are aged 15 to 29.

In nations like Kenya, young men with no prospects will resort to violence rather than quietly accept a future of failure.

With so many superfluous, frustrated young men, who are better fed and educated than ever before but have few prospects of finding a good job, nations with a youth bulge are likely to experience social upheaval.

In countries where large birth rates are combined with abject poverty and hunger, young men are much more likely to sink into lethargy.

But in nations like Kenya, young men with no prospects will resort to violence rather than quietly accept a future of failure.

Future Unrest

Given these figures, what may be more surprising in Kenya is not the violence, but the long periods of relative calm. This was partly due to the availability of uncultivated land for young men coming of age.

It would be even more surprising if Kenya quickly returns to internal harmony.

Over the next 15 years, some 8.1 million young Kenyan males will reach "fighting age" (15 to 29 years), compared to the 5.7 million in that bracket today.

With its unused land running out, Kenya may be overwhelmed by a wave of violence that matches those of its neighbors.

Iran's Choice of Education Is Associated with Decline in Fertility

Mohammed Jalal Abbasi-Shavazi, Wolfgang Lutz, Meimanat Hosseini-Chavoshi, and Samir K.C.

Mohammad Jalal Abbasi-Shavazi is head of the division of population research at the University of Tehran. Wolfgang Lutz is director of the Vienna Institute of Demography of the Austrian Academy of Sciences. Meimanat Hosseini-Chavoshi is a research associate at the Australian Demographic and Social Research Institute of the Australian National University. Samir K.C. is a research scholar with the World Population Program at IIASA [International Institute for Applied Systems Analysis], Laxenburg, Austria. In the following viewpoint, the authors note that the total fertility rate (TFR) in Iran dropped from seven children per woman in 1980 to 1.9 children per women in 2006. The authors conclude that by one standard "more than one-third of the actual fertility decline since [1980] can be attributed directly to changes in the composition of the reproductive age population by level of educational attainment."

As you read, consider the following questions:

1. According to Cochrane, what effects does education have on marriage and fertility?

Mohammed Jalal Abbasi-Shavazi, Wolfgang Lutz, Meimanat Hosseini-Chavoshi, and Samir K.C., "Education and the World's Most Rapid Fertility Decline in Iran," Interim Report IR-08-010, Laxenburg, Austria: International Institute of Applied Systems Analysis, 2008. Reproduced by permission.

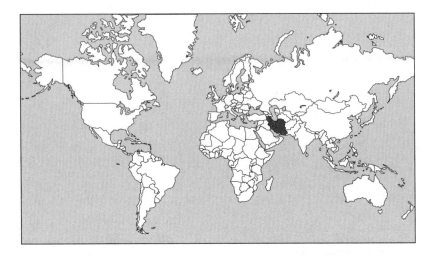

2. What was the difference in total fertility rate between rural and urban areas in 1980? In 2006?

3. What age group had the highest fertility rate in 1976? In 2006?

1. Introduction

Demographers tend to study all phenomena by age and sex. But there are other human characteristics that show great discriminatory power in explaining differential trends and on which good statistical information is available. Education is a prime candidate for this and it has been shown that explicitly considering education as a source of observed heterogeneity can add greatly to understanding the forces driving a phenomenon, in this case a very rapid fertility decline.

It is very common to associate changes in the education levels of women with changes in fertility levels. It is so conventional, in fact, that education plays a role in almost all theoretical approaches to the fertility transition. Education is said to provide access to modern ways of thinking, to provide confidence to engage in the modern world, to reduce infant and child mortality, to stimulate higher levels of gender equity within couple relationships, and to promote labor force participation of women in the cash economy, hence raising the opportunity cost of having children. The education of women may also lead to a greater emphasis on their part on the 'quality' of children as opposed to the quantity of children. Finally, education is a broad indicator of societal modernization (Lucas and Meyer 1994: 63-64). According to Cochrane (1979: 147) women's education is likely to raise the age at marriage and, in some countries, reduce the probability of ever marrying. Cochrane (1979: 9) noted that education is positively related to more favorable attitudes towards birth control, a greater knowledge of contraception, and husband-wife communication. Caldwell (1982: 315-320) stated that education influences fertility by a) reducing the benefits from children's work, b) increasing the costs of children, c) increasing the importance of the investment nature of children, d) speeding cultural change, and e) propagating Western middle-class values. As education levels increase, the educated woman is very likely to be married to an educated man and to be living in an educated society (Abbasi-Shavazi et al. 2003).

Education can be divided broadly into formal (through schooling) and informal (acquiring knowledge from various sources, including media, face-to-face contacts, etc). One of the main social changes in the 20th century and particularly over the past two decades has been the expansion of mass (formal) education in Iran. The literacy rate has increased dramatically in both urban and rural areas. . . . For example, the literacy rate for women aged 15-19 in urban areas increased from around 57 percent in 1966 to around 97 percent (almost universal) in 1996. The improvement in rural areas has been more dramatic, increasing from only 5 percent in 1966 to 86 percent in 1996. In 2006, around 98 percent of women aged 20-24 and 96 percent of women aged 25-29 in urban areas were literate as compared with 90 and 84 percent in rural areas, respectively.

In 1998, around 52 percent of those admitted to government universities were girls. The figure increased to 57 percent in 1999 and then to around 65 percent in 2007. These increases in educational attainment for Iranian girls mean that marriage and childbearing are often delayed into the early twenties. Studies suggest that aspirations and expectations of women in post-revolutionary Iran have also risen considerably (Shadi-Talab 2005; Abdollahyan 2004; Mir-Hosseini 2002; Kian-Thiebaut 2002). This has led to the improvement of the status of women at least within the family, and women have increased their role in family decision making. Increased literacy has contributed to women's confidence and has increased women's perceptions that they have options in many aspects of their lives, particularly women in rural areas who had been much constrained by past gender inequities (Hoodfar 1996: 35). Maternal education has also contributed to the reduction of infant mortality (Caldwell 1989; Cleland 1990), a factor which is conducive to higher child survival, and thus, reduces the demand for children.

In addition to formal schooling, informal education and knowledge has indirectly contributed to the reduction of fertility in Iran. The legitimization of family planning in post-revolutionary Iran paved the way for printing family planning brochures, teaching population education in high schools, holding workshops for young couples and other educational campaigns by the mass media. The rise in access to electricity, TV, radio, and transport and communication in remote areas of Iran has also increased knowledge and information of families at large. By 1996, the majority of rural communities had access to electricity, TV, radio and piped water (Abbasi-Shavazi 2000). The Literacy Movement was another organization created after the Revolution, aiming to instruct all illiterates above 10 years of age. The organization began its task in 1979 by dispatching volunteer school graduates as teachers to the villages. There were also some classes to instruct illiterate employees under 50 working in government offices, factories and workshops. The establishment of a health network system and health houses in rural areas diffused the idea of small family size and family planning. The system employed local girls and boys as health officers, Behvarz, who have had regular face-to-face contacts with women of childbearing ages to provide them with family planning information and services. The compulsory pre-marriage counseling was another way by which newly married couples have been able to gain information on contraceptives, STDs, and other issues related to maternal and child health care. In this paper, our main focus is on the impact of formal education and expansion of schooling on fertility decline in Iran....

Iran's Fertility Decline

Studies reveal that the changes in fertility in Iran during the late 1960s and early 1970s have been small. The total fertility rate (TFR) decreased from above 7.0 in 1966 (Amani 1970, 1996; Aghajanian and Mehryar 1999; Ladier-Fouladi 1997) to around 6.5 in 1976 (Mirzaie 2005). Due to socio-political changes as well as the revolutionary protests during the years preceding the 1979 Islamic Revolution, like many other government activities, the family planning program became inactive during the years 1977 to 1979. The TFR rose to 7.0 by 1980. However, Iran has experienced a phenomenal fall in fertility since the mid-1980s. The TFR declined from 7.0 in 1980 to around 5.6 in 1988 (Figure 4). The decline of fertility was slow until the new family planning program was officially inaugurated in 1989. The TFR fell sharply as of that time, dropping from around 5.6 in 1988 to around 2.8 in 1996, and to 2.2 in 2000 (Abbasi-Shavazi and McDonald 2006). Recent estimates of fertility indicate that the TFR declined to around 1.9 in 2006 (Abbasi-Shavazi and Nourollahi 2008).

The sharp fall of fertility in Iran since the mid-1980s deserves attention. That the decline occurred in an Islamic country is remarkable, particularly considering the sociopolitical context in Iran during and after the Islamic Revolution. Indeed, the decline of fertility (after the rise during the 1979 Islamic Revolution) started in the mid-1980s when there was no population or family planning policy. However, the decline accelerated with the reinstatement of the family planning program in 1989.

The similarity of the transition in both urban and rural areas is one the main features of the fertility transition in Iran. There was a considerable gap between the fertility in rural and urban areas, but the TFR in both rural and urban areas continued to decline by the mid-1990s, and the gap has narrowed substantially. In 1980, the TFR in rural areas was 8.4 while that of urban areas was 5.6. In other words, there was a gap of 2.8 children between rural and urban areas. In 2006, the TFR in rural and urban areas was 2.1 and 1.8, respectively (a difference of only 0.3 children).

Age-Specific Fertility Rates, 1972-2006

Figure 5 shows age-specific fertility for the period, 1976-2006. In 1976, the highest age-specific fertility rate was recorded for the age group 20-24 (283 per 1,000 women) followed by age groups 25-29 (268 per 1,000 women) and 30-34 (231 per 1,000 women). From 1976 to 1980, increases in fertility were evident for all age groups. However, during the first half of the 1980s, although the TFR remained high and nearly constant, the age pattern shifted towards later childbearing and the peak of childbearing occurred in the age group 25-29. The decreases in fertility at younger ages were matched by increases at older ages. Thus, Iranian women had a relatively early childbearing pattern in the first year of the revolution, consistent with the pronatalist ideology adopted by the government. This behavior did not last long, however, and as age at first marriage increased, fertility shifted to a relatively later childbearing pattern.

Female Literacy in Iran

Since the Iranian Revolution in 1979, female literacy has increased rapidly.

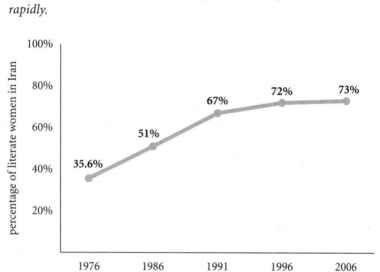

TAKEN FROM: Mike Dowling, "Female Literacy," *Mr.Dowling.com*, June 29, 2006. http://www.mrdowling.com; Nasrin Mosaffa, "Women's Empowerment in Iran: The Practice of Political Development," Tohoku University's *Research Group for Middle Eastern and Central Asian Studies*, August 22, 2000. http://mecas.cir.tohoku.ac.jp.

The figure depicts a remarkable fall in fertility in all age groups during 1986-1996. The rate of decline was slower afterwards, as there was less scope for further decline during this period. There was also an indication of a further shift towards delayed childbearing starting in 2000. By 2006 the peak of childbearing is observed in age group 25-29 which confirms a time lag between the first and second birth as well as the end of childbearing at parity 2 or 3 during the 1980s and 1990s (Hosseini-Chavoshi et al. 2006).

Age-specific fertility rates for rural and urban areas for the period 1976-2000 (data not presented here) reveal that, in general, the trends in age patterns of fertility for both rural and urban areas during the period were similar to those at the national level (Abbasi-Shavazi and McDonald 2005, 2006). The gaps between the TFRs in rural and urban areas had narrowed considerably by the end of the 1990s....

Discussion

A decline in the TFR of more than 5.0 in roughly two decades is a world record in fertility decline. This is even more surprising to many observers when one considers that it happened in one of the most Islamic societies. It forces the analyst to reconsider many of the usual stereotypes about religious fertility differentials. While in many industrialized countries the fertility of Muslim minority populations is significantly higher than that of the women belonging to the (mostly Christian) majority populations, this may not be due to religion per se, but rather to specific social and economic characteristics of the populations compared. In Austria, for example, the Muslim fertility level is higher by a factor of two. But the Muslim women living in Austria are mostly recent immigrants or descendents of immigrants from rural Anatolia. Their educational attainment is far below that of the average Austrian woman. It would be interesting to see how the religious differentials would turn out, if controlled for at the level of education.

But the Islamic Republic of Iran not only experienced the world's most rapid fertility transition, it was associated with a stunning increase in education and in particular female education. Young women in Iran today are almost as well educated as young men with an average of 8.4 years of schooling. This challenges another powerful stereotype, namely that Muslim societies discriminate against women for religious reasons. At least in Iran this does not seem to be the case with respect to education. And since education has been shown to be the most powerful long-term driver of emancipation, income and economic development (Lutz et al. 2008) there is reason for optimism concerning the future of Iran.

It is evident that the remarkable speed of fertility decline and the equally remarkable increase in female education are closely linked social trends. This paper has tried to provide a quantitative decomposition of the role that education played in the fertility decline. If the educational fertility differentials of 1980 are used as the standard, more than one-third of the actual fertility decline since then can be attributed directly to changes in the composition of the reproductive age population by level of educational attainment. The rest has been due to forces that brought down fertility rates among women at a given level of educational attainment. But although not measured in terms of the four formal education categories considered here, these drivers are likely to be associated with education in the broader sense. First, even in terms of formal education, within each of the four categories, women improved their education over time (higher mean years of schooling per category) which is likely to be associated with lower fertility. Second and more important, there are many channels of informal education and learning that contribute to value changes, changes in desired family size, more information and better access to family planning, and hence, directly or indirectly contribute to fertility decline. More research on these informal channels of education that presumably matter for fertility is clearly needed.

References

Abbasi-Shavazi, M.J. 2000. Effects of Marital Fertility and Nuptiality on Fertility Transition in the Islamic Republic of Iran. Working Papers in Demography, No. 84. Canberra: The Australian National University.

Abbasi-Shavazi, M.J. and P. McDonald. 2006. The fertility decline in the Islamic Republic of Iran, 1972–2000. *Asian Population Studies* 2(3): 217–237.

Abbasi-Shavazi, M.J. and P. McDonald. 2005. National and Provincial-level Fertility Trends in Iran: 1972–2000. Working Paper in Demography, No. 94. Canberra: The Australian National University.

Abbasi-Shavazi, M.J. and T. Nourollahi. 2008. Recent Fertility Trends in Iran: Application of the Own-children Method to the 2006 Census. Paper presented at the 4th Conference of the Population Association of Iran, Tehran, March 4–5, 2008.

Abbasi-Shavazi, M.J., P. McDonald, and M. Hosseini-Chavoshi. 2008. Modernization and the cultural practice of consanguineous marriage: Case study in four province of Iran. *Journal of Biosocial Science* [online publication]: 1–23.

Abbasi-Shavazi, M.J., P. McDonald, and M. Hosseini-Chavoshi. 2003. Changes in Family, Fertility Behavior and Attitudes in Iran. Working Paper in Demography No. 88. Canberra: Australian National University.

Abdollahyan, H. 2004. The generation gap in contemporary Iran. *Journal of Welt Trends* 44: 78–85.

Aghajanian, A. and A. Mehryar. 1999. Fertility transition in the Islamic Republic of Iran: 1967–1996. *Asia-Pacific Population Journal* 14(1): 21–42.

Amani, M. 1996. An attempt at the historical outlook of the trends of births and death rates and study of the stage of demographic transition in Iran [in Persian]. *Journal of Population* 13–14: 71–83.

Amani, M. 1970. Births and fertility in Iran, division of population research [in Persian]. Tehran, Iran: Institute for Social Studies and Research, University of Tehran.

Caldwell, J.C. 1989. Mass education as a determinant of mortality decline. Pages 101–109 in J.C. Caldwell and G.

Santow (eds), *Selected Readings in the Cultural, Social and Behavioral Determinants of Health.* Health Transition Series, No. 1. Canberra: Australian National University.

Caldwell, J. 1982. *Theory of Fertility Decline.* London: Academic Press.

Cleland, J. 1990. Maternal education and child survival: Further evidence and explanation. Pages 400–419 in J.C. Caldwell, S. Findley, P. Caldwell, G. Santow, W. Cosford, J. Braid, and D. Broers-Freeman (eds.), *What We Know About Health Transition: The Cultural, Social and Behavioral Determinants of Health.* Proceedings of an International Workshop, Canberra, May 1989. Health Transition Series, No. 2. Canberra: The Australian National University.

Cochrane, S.H. 1979. *Fertility and Education: What Do We Really Know?* Baltimore, MD: John Hopkins University Press.

Hoodfar, H. 1996. Bargaining with fundamentalism: Women and the politics of population control in Iran. *Reproductive Health Matters* 8: 30–40.

Hosseini-Chavoshi, M., P. McDonald, and M.J. Abbasi-Shavazi. 2006. The Iranian fertility decline, 1981–1999: An application of the synthetic parity progression ratio method. *Population* 61(5–6): 701–718.

Kian-Thiebaut, A. 2002. Women and the making of civil society in post-Islamist Iran. Pages 56–73 in Eric Hooglund (ed.), *Twenty Years of Islamic Revolution: Political and Social Transition in Iran since 1979.* Syracuse, NY: Syracuse University Press.

Ladier-Fouladi, M. 1997. The fertility transition in Iran. *Population: An English Selection* 9: 191–214.

Lucas, D., and P. Meyer. 1994. The background to fertility. Pages 56–68 in D. Lucas and P. Meyer (eds.), *Beginning Population Studies.* 2nd edition. Canberra: The Australian National University.

Lutz, W., J. Crespo Cuaresma, and W. Sanderson. 2008. The demography of educational attainment and economic growth. *Science* 319: 1047–1048.

Mir-Hosseini, Z. 2002. Religious modernists and the "woman question." Pages 74–95 in Eric Hooglund (ed.), *Twenty Years of Islamic Revolution: Political and Social Transition in Iran since 1979.* Syracuse, NY: Syracuse University Press.

Mirzaie, M. 2005. Swings in fertility limitations in Iran. *Critique: Critical Middle Eastern Studies* 14(1): 25–33.

Shadi-Talab, J. 2005. Iranian women: Rising expectations. *Critique: Critical Middle Eastern Studies* 14(1): 35–55.

Egypt Struggles to Find Socially Acceptable Ways to Reduce Fertility

Will Rasmussen

Will Rasmussen has written for Reuters and many publications, including the Beirut Daily Star. *In the following viewpoint, he reports that Egypt's population is growing rapidly, putting serious strains on fertile land and on water, especially from the Nile River. However, the Egyptian government has found it very difficult to limit the growth. Egyptians, Rasmussen says, are very resistant to birth control; they see large families as a source of strength. There are also Muslim religious objections to birth control. Without widespread popular support, Rasmussen indicates, the government feels unable to push through birth control measures—such as lowering maternity benefits for large families—which have been successful in nearby countries such as Iran. Egypt, Rasmussen concludes, may be part of a wave of poor countries with rapidly growing populations that will have a major impact on world demography.*

As you read, consider the following questions:

1. What percentage of Egyptians are younger than 15?
2. How many people per square kilometer live in some districts of Cairo?
3. Do Muslim clerics allow contraception?

Will Rasmussen, "Egypt Fights to Stem Population Growth," Reuters, July 2, 2008. Reproduced by permission.

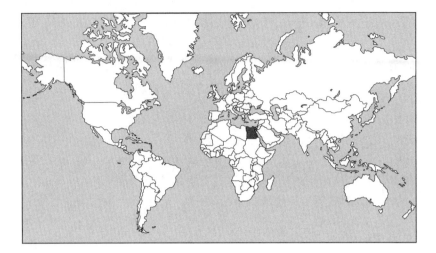

Red and white banners along Nile bridges and Cairo streets
this month [July 2008] were Egypt's latest effort to curb
an increasingly pressing problem: a population growing faster
than the economy can support.

Since President Hosni Mubarak took office in 1981, the
population has nearly doubled. But most of the country's 76
million people are squashed in urban areas near the Nile, in
an area roughly the size of Switzerland, which is home to just
7.5 million.

"Before you add another baby, make sure his needs are se-
cured," ran the slogan, adding to a string of campaigns over
30 years to encourage family planning. Mubarak told a
government-sponsored population conference that cutting
population growth was urgent.

---

*According to the United Nations, the poor are set to be
more and more numerous by 2050.*

Rising Rates of Poverty

With about one fifth of the population living on less than $1
a day and food and fuel prices lifting inflation to a 19-year

high, discontent is mounting. But beyond domestic concerns, Egypt could become a poster-child for a global trend.

According to the United Nations, the poor are set to be more and more numerous by 2050 and many will be living in towns as the world population climbs to a total of 9.2 billion. Essentially all the growth will be in less developed countries.

Egypt—where the divide between rich and poor is stark and resistance to targeted birth control common—shows how that could happen.

"Impossible," said Cairo taxi-driver and father-of-five Mohammed Ahmed, waving a cigarette in the air for emphasis when asked about Mubarak's appeal to slow population growth. "That is for God to decide."

Around 38 percent of Egyptians are younger than 15, and according to the World Bank, women make up only around 22 percent of the labour force, so the incentive for birth control is weak.

Population growth has remained stubbornly high at around 2 percent for the last decade and the fertility rate, at about 3.1 children per woman—compared with 2.1 in the United States—has also been stable.

Lacking the oil reserves of their Gulf Arab neighbours to fund investment. Egypt's recent economic growth at around 7 percent has not been steady enough to build a significant middle class.

Government Baffled

"The population explosion is a crisis the government doesn't know how to handle," said Milad Hanna, a former member of parliament and a columnist at the state-owned newspaper *al-Ahram.*

While lamenting the strain on the country's limited resources—especially of water and fertile land in a country where rainfall is almost zero—the government has avoided using incentives or punitive policies to modify behaviour.

Water in the Desert

Egypt is facing a population boom in its already over-crowded Nile corridor. It has no choice but to move into desert lands and redirect people and agriculture. Over the past 50 years, the country has invested enormous resources to divert water from the Nile into desert areas.

Yet how can desert expansion be sustained when Egypt's very limited water supply is consumed virtually for free? Developers continue to set up five-star resorts in the Sinai that rely on water pumped in from the Nile.

VOAnews.com,
"Egypt Uses Water Resources to Make Desert Bloom,"
August 1, 2006. www.voanews.com.

Firm measures such as restricting maternity benefits for those with large families, which helped Iran sharply slow its population growth during the 1990s, would be politically dangerous in Egypt, where there have already been protests over food shortages, said Hanna.

Egyptians, especially in the countryside, view large families as a source of economic strength. Many will continue bearing children until they have a boy.

Egypt is not about to legalise abortion, which has helped Tunisia bring down its fertility levels, and vasectomy, commonly practised in Iran, is barely heard of in Egypt.

Egyptians, especially in the countryside, view large families as a source of economic strength. Many will continue bearing children until they have a boy.

"The population will continue to grow and the government can only make an appeal," Hanna said.

Growing Troubles

The outlook for both Egypt and the region will be grave if the most populous Arab country continues to grow at current rates, Egyptian and U.N. officials say.

"The consequences are a real deterioration in the quality of life and in agricultural land per person," said Magued Osman, chairman of the cabinet's Information and Decision Support Center. "We are depending heavily on imported food items and this will increase."

If levels of growth don't slow, Mubarak says Egypt's population could double to 160 million by 2050. But Egypt's government hopes it can be stabilised at 100 million "More than that will be difficult," Osman said.

In the absence of significant rainfall the greatest constraint is Egypt's dependence on the waters of the Nile, for which it has to compete against rival demands upstream.

Egypt already uses more than its quota of Nile water, 55.5 billion cubic metres a year, and might have to cut back on consumption if Sudan uses more or if other Nile Basin countries, such as Ethiopia and Uganda, divert more water for themselves.

In a 1959 treaty, Egypt and Sudan agreed to take almost all the Nile's flow for themselves, leaving out other Nile basin states, who have not agreed to respect it.

In the meantime the Egyptian government is moving Nile water deep into the desert, both for urban development and to water reclaimed agricultural land to grow more food.

Moving out of the Nile valley is the obvious choice to relieve the crowding in places like Cairo, where some districts hold 41,000 people per square km (100,000 per square mile). Manhattan, by comparison, has about 27,000 people per square km.

But some experts question whether a $70 billion government plan to reclaim 3.4 million acres of desert over the next 10 years—which Egypt continues to push ahead with—is feasible given constraints on water.

Tens of thousands of Egyptians a year try to reach Europe, Libya, or the Gulf countries in search of jobs at wages that they cannot find at home. Many die at sea on the way to Europe.

Growth Pushes Emigration

Ziad Rifai, Egypt representative for the United Nations Population Fund, said continuing high population growth in Egypt could affect neighbouring countries.

"If the general welfare of the people goes below a certain threshold, it affects stability in the region and it affects migration," he said. "The worse the conditions get, the easier it is for extremism to flourish."

Tens of thousands of Egyptians a year try to reach Europe, Libya, or the Gulf countries in search of jobs at wages that they cannot find at home. Many die at sea on the way to Europe.

Mubarak tends to avoid mentioning a specific number of children but the government says it prefers a family with two.

Announcing a number would be wrong, said Ali Abdelatif, 34, a security guard who supports two children on about $70 per month.

"My wife gets pregnant very easily," he said, smiling. "So it's okay to use birth control for the sake of her health, but specifying a number of kids—that is forbidden."

Although clerics in the country, which is about 90 percent Muslim, generally allow contraception, many disagree with targeting a specific number of children.

Birth control for fear of poverty or to prevent conception permanently is unlawful under Islam, according to a fatwa, or Islamic edict on Islam Online, a popular forum for Islamic rulings.

"From a religious point of view I am against the call of President Mubarak," said Salim Awwa, secretary general of the influential International Union for Muslim Scholars. "The state is not God and the state is not the creator. We should not try to limit the number of children."

Chinese People Support State-Enforced Population Control and Abortion

Nie Jing-Bao

Nie Jing-Bao is senior lecturer at the Bioethics Centre, University of Otago, New Zealand. In the following viewpoint, Nie presents his research on attitudes concerning China's birth control policy, especially the 'one-child' policy, which imposes hefty fines on couples who have more than one child, and in some cases even forces women to have abortions. Nie found that the people he interviewed overwhelmingly supported population control, up to and including the use of coerced abortions. This is because, Nie says, most Chinese believe that overpopulation is a serious problem for China. They believe this, Nie argues, in large part because state-run media says that it is a serious problem, and there is no public forum to debate whether this is true or not. So while Chinese support for state family planning is real, Nie avers, it is built upon state control of the media, and might shift radically if real debate or freedom of speech were allowed.

As you read, consider the following questions:

1. What percentage of those surveyed by Nie thought that the one-child policy was beneficial to the country?

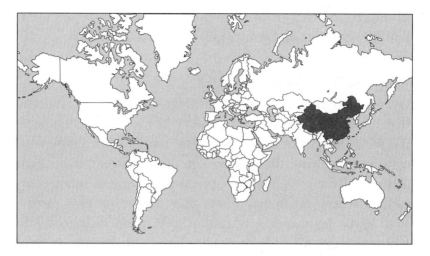

2. What is one of the three reasons that urban women in China give for supporting the one-child policy, as reported by Nie?

3. Since when has the state-media in China pushed the message that overpopulation is a serious problem?

The Chinese birth control program is, by and large, successful; the population growth rate in China has been reduced to below 2% within two decades. The arrival of the day when China's population reaches 1.2 billion has been postponed by about a decade. This remarkable achievement would be unimaginable without the strong will and control by the state and the efficiency of its bureaucracy in implementing the state policies. It would also be impossible without the popular consensus that rapid population growth and overpopulation constitute such a serious social problem in China that strict state intervention is necessary.

A number of paradoxes exist in China's birth control program. One of the most striking is the coexistence of the wide acceptance and even strong support on one side and the persistent and even violent resistance on the other side. Without making some sense of these paradoxes, it would be impossible

191

to understand the socio-cultural dimensions of coerced abortion in particular and contemporary China in general.

Support for National Policy

Over and over again, the Chinese government has claimed that the national birth control policy has won and is enjoying the wide support of the people. The results of my survey ... confirm this claim; that is, the national birth control policy is endorsed by a great majority of people. Chinese participants in the survey—no matter where they resided or their profession, Party membership, education level, gender, or even religious beliefs—overwhelmingly believed in the necessity of controlling the rapid population growth in China and supported the national family planning program in general and the "one-child" policy in particular. In fact, this was the area with the strongest consensus among all the participants surveyed and interviewed. Even Catholics, who clearly oppose abortion in general, were somehow more cautious about population control and the "one-child" policy than participants from other groups, but still were considerably supportive. Ninety-four percent of the participants in the survey agreed that the one-child-per-couple policy is beneficial to the country; 82% agreed that the policy is beneficial to the individual and the family. Moreover, Chinese participants in all samples supported "very strongly" the necessity of taking eugenic (*yousheng*) [regulating birth so "good" offspring are produced] measures to improve the quality of China's population. In other words, national family planning program, whose main task is not only to control the rapid increase of population but also to improve the quality of the population, was highly supported by all groups, including rural people, urban residents, intellectuals, university students, doctors, overseas students and scholars, and even Catholics.

The interviews with physicians who provided family planning medical service and with women who had abortions further confirmed this wide acceptance and strong support of the Chinese people for the birth control policy. Almost all of thirty doctors [interviewed] were proud of directly participating in the family planning program—a good and great cause—because they believed they were serving the whole society by helping slow the rapid population growth. The most frequent reason mentioned for their abortions by the thirty women who had had them was that the policy did not allow the pregnancy to continue. But, . . . it is incorrect to interpret this to mean that they disagreed with the population policy. On the contrary, most women supported and accepted the birth control program, though they were less supportive than the doctors.

Chinese participants in the survey . . . overwhelmingly believed in the necessity of controlling the rapid population growth in China and supported the national family planning program.

Concern About Overpopulation

In my fieldwork, I encountered people from all walks of life—peasants, urban residents, medical professionals, university professors, hotel workers, taxi drivers—who were forthright in expressing their concerns about overpopulation and voicing their approval for the national population policy. An official at a provincial institution said to me on his own initiative: "Even though I am a member of the Communist Party and a governmental, I oppose many policies of the Party and the state. But I support the family planning policy from my heart."

There were reservations and criticisms regarding the national birth control policy, most notably among overseas Chinese and doctors. But . . . these reservations and criticisms targeted not so much the population policy as the methods of implementing this policy. In other words, the necessity of a national birth control policy was rarely questioned.

Number of Children Desired by Chinese Women, 2001

More than half of the 39,600 Chinese women surveyed wanted more than one child. Nonetheless, support for the one-child policy in China is high, suggesting some women are willing to put aside personal desires for what they see as a greater social good.

Variable	No children	1 child	2 children	3 or more children	No preference	Mean no. of children preferred
			percent			
Age (yr)						
15–24	1.9	50.0	44.0	2.1	2.3	1.5
25–34	0.8	37.0	57.0	4.5	0.7	1.7
≥35	0.9	27.0	63.0	9.0	0.4	1.8
Place of residence						
Rural area	0.4	30.0	61.0	7.5	1.2	1.8
Urban area	3.1	52.0	43.0	1.5	0.9	1.4
Educational level						
Primary school	0.4	21.0	66.0	12.0	0.9	1.9
Middle or high school	2.1	47.0	46.0	3.9	1.6	1.5
College	4.0	49.0	45.0	2.3	0.8	1.4
Total for all women	1.1	35.0	57.0	5.8	1.1	1.7

TAKEN FROM: Therese Hesketh and Zhu Wei Xing, "The Effect of China's One-Child Policy After 25 Years," *The New England Journal of Medicine Online*, vol. 353, no. 11, September 15, 2005, pp. 1171–76. http://content.nejm.org.

No item in the questionnaire is directly about coerced abortion caused by the birth control policies or about the morality of coerced abortion. But the survey results do indicate that most survey respondents, with the Catholic sample as the only exception, agreed with the statement that it is sometimes necessary to force a woman to have an abortion. . . . The evident support for coerced abortion, at least under some circumstances, together with the overwhelmingly strong support for the national family planning program, suggest that coerced terminations *may* be approved and accepted by a large majority of Chinese as one legitimate means of implementing the population policy.

Is Support Genuine?

While Chinese support for the national family planning program is widespread and there is general approval for employing coerced abortion to effectively implement the national policy, crucial questions are raised: How genuine, if genuine at all, is this strong consensus among Chinese people, or the agreement between the Party–state and the people? If the data are reliable, then why do the overwhelming majority of Chinese accept and support the national birth control program? One can explain all this consensus away by saying that Chinese people were either simply afraid of saying what they really believed or merely giving lip service to the birth control policies, or both. In other words, the consensus or agreement was a result of political repression and enforced silence and thus said nothing about the genuine views of Chinese people. However, according to my judgments and observations, this factor is far from the most significant because the survey and interviewing results in general are reliable, because participants in the survey disagreed with several other officially approved statements, and because different and dissenting views on other issues were often expressed. That is to say, I believe that Chinese participants' expressed opinions on population control—accepting and supporting the birth control program—are basically genuine.

It is important to understand that overpopulation is an obvious and serious social problem for Chinese people. People living in China, especially in cities, readily perceive and suffer the consequences of overpopulation, every day and everywhere. As a result, Chinese have reached a "conscientious acceptance" of the need to limit family size. The phrase "conscientious acceptance" was used by Cecilia N. Milwertz to account for the fact that most urban women, despite their clearly stated preference for two children, accept the "one-child" family policy. Milwertz has convincingly shown that city district women widely accept a policy that does not necessarily correspond to their own fertility preference—more than one child. In other words, it is incorrect to take the preference for two children as an accurate measure of nonacceptance of the policy. For "acceptance transcends individual and family fertility preference" and "compliance is not necessarily perceived as something negative." Among reasons urban women give for accepting the policy are (1) given the present demographic and economic situation in China, they agree with the official rationale for the necessity of a national population control program; (2) they have neither the funds nor the energy to support more than one child, in spite of their personal preference for two or more children; and (3) they want to respond to the call of the state. According to Milwertz, "conscientious acceptance" (*zijue jieshou*) "connotes the exercise of self-control and is related to the political consciousness in terms of acting according to the prescribed norm without having to be persuaded." The logic or "cultural meaning" of conscientious acceptance, compliance, self-control, or self-sacrifice is not necessarily perceived as something negative. Milwertz, by focusing on the nondemographic consequences of the "one-child" family policy—how women handle it "in their everyday life context"—has indicated the subtlety of coercion in the Chinese sociocultural context.

People living in China, especially in cities, readily perceive and suffer the consequences of overpopulation, every day and everywhere.

Genuine, but Forced

However, that Chinese people were expressing their true feelings and opinions does not necessarily mean that their agreement with the official policies is genuine in the sense that it is ethically valid. Or it must be emphasized that it is a mistake to see the extremely strong consensus as an agreement reached after sufficient public discussions. In fact, to a great degree the consensus is not a genuine but a forced one, created by continuous governmental propaganda and powerful public education. Since the late 1970s, the state-run media have hammered home the dual message that overpopulation is a grave social problem in itself and that many other problems such as food shortages and deficits in housing and education have resulted from uncontrolled population growth. Meanwhile, different or opposing views are hardly heard in public and official discourse. Scant literature, if any at all, argues that population is not a severe social problem and that, if it is, strict national policies do not necessarily constitute the best solution. The dissident voices are usually, if not always, repressed even before they are fully developed. Not informed by different perspectives, Chinese people are left no choice but to accept the government views that overpopulation is one of the biggest social problems, if not the biggest, in China and that the only way out is through direct and strict state interference. Hence, strong propaganda on the one hand and the suppression of dissident perspectives on the other hand have actually forced Chinese people to believe that, in the face of the serious condition of overpopulation, there is no way out but the present national policies.

Consequently, the strong acceptance of and support for the national birth control policy is itself a paradox. It is based on Chinese people's awareness of the problem of overpopulation, but the nature of this problem and the best social policies for addressing it are far from sufficiently deliberated and discussed by the public. Even if the Chinese strong consensus on the population problem and the birth control program is a "conscientious acceptance," it is a misinformed or, at best, an insufficiently informed one. From the angle of the efficiency, the state can exercise much better control over people by controlling and manipulating information available to them, rather than directly suppressing their thought and speech.

To Control Population Growth, Peru Forcibly Sterilized Women

Ángel Páez

Ángel Páez is an award-winning Peruvian journalist. He is the founder and director of Peru's first investigative reporting team at the newspaper La Republica. *He has reported on numerous cases of government corruption and military abuses. In the following selection, he reports that Hilaria Supa Huamán was elected to the Peruvian Congress in 2006. Supa had long campaigned to prosecute those responsible for a program of coerced sterilization that took place in the late 1990s, under the administration of President Alberto Fujimori. The program resulted in the sterilization of more than 360,000 women, many of whom suffered lasting pain and health complications. One of those in charge of the program was Alejandro Aguinaga, Supa's fellow Congressman and the former health minister under Fujimori. According to Páez, Aguinaga argued that the sterilization issue should be dropped, while Supa hoped that those responsible, including Aguinaga, would be punished.*

As you read, consider the following questions:

1. During what time period was the Voluntary Surgical Contraception (VSC) program implemented?

Ángel Páez, "Rights-Peru: Forcibly Sterilized Women Gain Voice in Congress," IPS, July 10, 2006. http://ipsnews.net. Reproduced by permission.

2. According to the parliamentary investigation, how did the Fujimori administration encourage doctors to sterilize women?

3. How many deaths were linked to VSC, according to the investigating committee?

Congressman-elect Alejandro Aguinaga, a former health minister during the Alberto Fujimori administration (1990–2000), as of Jul. 28 [2006] will have to snare the legislative chamber with rural activist Hilaria Supa Huamán, who has denounced him for promoting the forced sterilisation of hundreds of thousands of Peruvian women.

Supa, who will occupy a seat representing Union for Peru—the party that supported the presidential candidacy of nationalist Ollanta Humala—formally accused Aguinaga, elected by the pro-Fujimori Alliance for the Future, of promoting a forced sterilisation programme which deprived 363,000 Peruvian women of their right to motherhood.

The case is currently in the hands of prosecutor Héctor Villar, who specialises in human rights. Sources at his office told IPS [Inter Press Service] that the magistrate is detailing the responsibility of the former health authorities in order to present charges.

When Supa lodged the accusation during Fujimori's administration, she never imagined that her leadership in defence of the rights of women in Cusco, in the south of the country, would take her so far. Today, this poor, indigenous Quechua-speaking mother is a member of Congress, just like Aguinaga.

Aguinaga Argues That Sterilization Is in the Past

Aguinaga said he could not recall who Supa was when IPS asked him about the rural women's leader from Cusco.

"I have just heard that she has been elected to Congress," he said. "No doubt we will have the opportunity to talk. What Peru needs now is development policies and not to keep harping on about the same things (the forced sterilisations), that have already been cleared up and shelved."

IPS told the former minister that a prosecutor is investigating the case and is about to bring charges, and that Supa would propose in Congress that those responsible for implementing the VSC (Voluntary Surgical Contraception) programme should be punished.

[Aguinaga] received us, but he denied everything. He said that the programme was of benefit to the poorest. We showed him testimonies, documents, proof. We even wept in front of him, but he paid no attention.

"As far as I'm concerned, the matter is closed," said Aguinaga. "We have to take action on issues of importance to the country, like the maternal mortality rate which continues to be high. Reproductive health is the priority now."

Aguinaga also said he was unaware of the status of the investigation he is subjected to by the human rights prosecutor. "I do not know what the situation is."

Sterilization Was Unsafe and Involuntary

But Supa is not about to let the past be forgotten. From 1996 to 2000, with the aim of drastically lowering the birth rate in Peru's most impoverished areas, Fujimori implemented the Voluntary Surgical Contraception (VSC) programme. Medical VSC brigades were dispatched to every corner of the country, including the southern Cusco town of Anta, near the rural community of Ollacocha, where Supa hails from.

After surgery, six of Supa's neighbours experienced terrible pain as a result of the ligation of their fallopian tubes. Supa recorded their testimonies, and those of other women in nearby communities who had undergone VSC, and she discovered that in Anta province, the Health Ministry teams were recruiting rural women with false promises or through intimidation.

Supa's neighbours elected her secretary general of the Anta Women's Federation, which launched a campaign against forced sterilisation in the entire Cusco region. In 1999, Supa travelled to Lima for an interview with the then health minister, Alejandro Aguinaga.

"He received us, but he denied everything. He said that the programme was of benefit to the poorest. We showed him testimonies, documents, proof. We even wept in front of him, but he paid no attention. He was very indifferent," Supa told IPS. The sterilisations continued until November 2000, when Fujimori fled to Japan and his health minister, along with the rest of the cabinet, resigned.

The 1994 International Conference on Population and Development, to which Peru is a party, established that all persons have the right to freely choose the number, timing and spacing of their children, and the states party to the agreement are committed to upholding that right.

Between 2001 and 2003, the Peruvian legislative Congress investigated Fujimori's family planning programme. It documented cases in which women had died as a result of side ef-

Two Peruvian Women

Angelica Leiva, . . . a 30-year-old woman who says that, alone and without her husband to help her decide what to do, she was forced to agree to sterilization during a government campaign. The surgery was botched: Only one fallopian tube was ligated and consequently she suffered an ectopic pregnancy [a dangerous complication of pregnancy]. Leiva says she was given no postoperative care. . . .

Auristela Melgar, a 41-year-old mother of eight, says the PMOH [Peruvian Ministry of Health] pressured her to be sterilized three years ago. Recently she was required to sit through three hours of lecture about the importance of family planning in exchange for a month's worth of cereal and dried milk to feed her children. Melgar told health workers she already had been sterilized, but the U.S. food was withheld from the children until she submitted to the lectures.

Catherine Edwards, "Human Rights—Poor Women Charge Forced Sterilization," Insight on the News, 2000. http://web.mit.edu.

fects of VSC, and determined that the authorities had instructed the medical brigades to sterilise minimum quotas of women in exchange for government benefits.

A first charge sheet, accusing Fujimori and his ministers of genocide, was thrown out because of mistakes in the categorisation of the crime.

The Investigation of Forced Sterilization Moves Forward

However, another parliamentary group, led by congresswoman Dora Núñez Dávila, reopened the case and concluded that crimes against the life and integrity of persons had been committed.

The group also acquired evidence that the Ministry of Health had paid cash "incentives" to doctors and their teams for every woman they sterilised, and that Fujimori's administration distributed food to community dining halls according to the number of women who had "volunteered" for VSC.

The programme was supported by the Peruvian armed forces, who were ordered to provide "security" for the medical brigades. The investigation involved three former health ministers, including Aguinaga, and several other officials. Aguinaga was deputy minister of health from 1994 on, and head of the portfolio from 1999 until the fall of the Fujimori regime.

Aguinaga "must pay for his crimes," Supa told IPS. "I still receive complaints from many sterilised women. They have been abandoned by the government, and by their families. They are still in pain. They can't work. Nobody is looking out for them. They have not been compensated for what was done to them. We have testimonies from more than 300 women in Cusco region who were affected."

When IPS asked Aguinaga whether he thought that the victims of the VSC programme deserved at least an apology from him, he replied: "All these years we have been dealing with the same thing, and I suppose that at some point I will talk to the lady (Hilaria Supa). I repeat, instead of harping on about the same thing (the investigation of forced sterilisation), we need development policies. The indicators are very bad."

I still receive complaints from many sterilised women. They have been abandoned by the government, and by their families. They are still in pain. They can't work. Nobody is looking out for them.

According to the report by the congressional investigating committee describing the abuses committed by the Fujimori administration, "Most of the population at which the (VSC) programme was aimed was illiterate and their native language was not Spanish, (but) the papers (the women) had to sign giving consent to the surgical contraception procedure were in Spanish."

"At the so-called 'health festivals', everything from sporting activities to surgical procedures went on, and the aim was to carry out mass VSC. On a single field day, up to 90 people could—and were expected to—be sterilised. The medical personnel who took part in the festivals tried to justify their behaviour, saying they were threatened that if they did not fulfil their work they would receive demerits or even be dismissed," the report said.

According to the investigating committee's document, there have been 18 deaths related to VSC. Between 1990 and 2001, 363,000 women were subjected to sterilisation, "the years of greatest intensity for this type of operation being 1995, 1997 and 1998."

Supa Still Hopes Those Responsible Will Be Punished

The period of constitutional pre-trial protection enjoyed by Fujimori and his ministers—proceedings in the Legislative branch before a trial in the Judiciary—ended in 2005, so the congressional investigation has been handed over to the National Prosecutor's office.

The parliamentary committee recommended that the alleged perpetrators be tried for the crimes of torture, kidnapping, serious injury and conspiracy to commit crimes.

Supa is optimistic that justice will be done, and says that it is only a matter of time.

"In Congress I'll make Aguinaga remember what he did," said Supa, her Spanish markedly influenced by Quechua, her mother tongue. "When we complained in Lima that many women were suffering pain because of the operations, the authorities told us that that wasn't due to the tubal ligations, but because we were dirty, ignorant and lazy. No more of that!"

Supa, who was among the 1,000 women nominated worldwide en masse for the Nobel Peace Prize in 2005, does not harbour ill-feeling, but she longs for justice: "For my people, for my children, for my ayllu (community, in Quechua), I will not rest until those responsible pay for what they did. Forced sterilisation will not remain unpunished."

In this battle, Aguinaga and Supa will meet face to face.

Britain Faces Dangerous Cultural Changes as Immigrants Cause Population Growth

Robert Whelan

Robert Whelan is the deputy director of Civitas, a British think tank, and is the author of Helping the Poor: Friendly Visiting, Dole Charities and Dole Queues. *In the following viewpoint, Whelan says that doomsayers like Thomas Malthus, who believed that population would outpace food supplies, have always been wrong in the past. For that reason, Whelan says, he has long believed that population growth is nothing to fear. However, Whelan says, he now believes there is a difference between natural population growth and immigration. The first, he says, is regulated by individual parents who know how many children they can raise. But immigration has no such regulation, Whelan believes, and it can therefore put great strains on a society. For example, Whelan says immigration can overwhelm transportation and education systems, and it can drive down wages. Most dangerously, Whelan feels, immigrants from some nations do not share British beliefs about freedom of speech and human rights.*

As you read, consider the following questions:

1. Why did Stanley Jeavons believe that the Industrial Revolution would grind to a halt?

Robert Whelan, "A State Struggling to Cope with 77 Million People," *Daily Telegraph*, August 28, 2008. www.telegraph.co.uk. Reproduced by permission.

2. Who was Julian Simon?

3. What does Eurostat predict that Britain's population will be by 2060?

In his *Essay on Population*, published in 1798, the Rev Thomas Malthus took a very gloomy view of the prospects for the nation if people continued to have large families.

A high birthrate, he extrapolated, would lead to population growth, that would outstrip the food supply, until famine acted as a corrective.

When he was writing, the population of Britain was eight million. It is now 61 million and that famine hasn't happened.

No Apocalypse

Perhaps the most famous thing about Malthus is that he was spectacularly wrong about food production. He argued that population increases geometrically—2,4,8,16—while food production increases arithmetically—1,2,3,4. Why he made this assumption no one knows. It wasn't true in 1798 and it certainly isn't true now.

Since Malthus, there have been many more scares about resources running out. The 19th-century economist Stanley

Jeavons predicted that the industrial revolution would grind to a halt because of the exhaustion of coal mines: he failed to foresee the emergence of other sources of energy.

Then, in [1972], the Club of Rome produced its famous report *The Limits to Growth* which said much the same thing about other natural resources. It contained a table showing estimated dates for the exhaustion of major resources. All of which have long passed.

In 1980, the American economist Julian Simon became so frustrated by the doomsday predictions that he made a bet with the principal doom-monger, Paul Ehrlich, on the actual scarcity of resources.

They compiled a notional basket of $1,000-worth of natural resources and agreed that if at the end of 10 years the basket was worth more than $1,000—which would indicate scarcity—then Julian would pay Ehrlich the difference. When the bet matured in 1990 the resources were worth $424.

[Economist] Julian [Simon]'s view was that, if the right political institutions were in place . . . more people would equate with a higher standard of living, because more people mean larger markets . . . and higher levels of consumption.

No Limit?

By this time, I had become involved with Julian in running an organisation called the Committee on Population and the Economy, which argued that population growth was nothing to fear.

Julian's view was that, if the right political institutions were in place to allow people to exercise their talents, more people would equate with a higher standard of living, because more people mean larger markets, lower unit costs, and higher levels of consumption.

Resources would never run out. Furthermore, Julian made no distinction between population growth resulting from high birthrates or from immigration, believing in a completely open-borders policy.

I hope I will not cause his departed spirit any disquiet if I say that I have now moved away from my original whole-hearted support of his position.

Parents Regulate Children

It seems to me there is an enormous difference between growth that results from parents deciding to have large families and that which results from virtually uncontrolled mass immigration such as we have had in Britain since 1997.

When parents have children, it creates pressures on resources, but, in the main, these pressures fall on the parents. Parents pretty much know how many children they can love and care for.

The huge increase in population in this country occurred during the 19th century when the benefits of scientific advance, the industrial revolution and the opening up of global markets gave everyone, but especially the poor, opportunities they had never had before—like seeing most of their children survive.

When people found that they didn't need 10 children to be sure of two surviving, they had fewer children. And when they feel their country is pretty full, they opt for smaller families.

Population growth and rising standards of living went together in Britain, as in many other parts of the world.

However, parents make decisions about family size based on their perceptions of society. As that society changes, so does family size.

Immigrants to Britain 2005–2006

	Citizenship	Immigration *Thousands*
1	British	177
2	Poland	124
3	India	104
4	Pakistan	49
5	China	49
6	Australia	48
7	South Africa	41
8	Germany	36
9	USA	32
10	New Zealand	24

TAKEN FROM: "Migration: UK Emigration reaches 400,000 in 2006," *National Statistics Online*, May 20, 2008. http://www.statistics.gov.uk.

When people found that they didn't need 10 children to be sure of two surviving, they had fewer children. And when they feel their country is pretty full, they opt for smaller families.

The birthrate in the UK has been below replacement level for 30 years now, although the overall size of the population has continued to grow.

This used to be because of increasing life expectancy, but the growth is now largely because of unprecedented levels of immigration.

Immigration Strains Resources

The scenario outlined by Eurostat, under which Britain will become the most populous country in Europe by 2060 with a population of 77 million, is not a cheerful one for most of us, as that increase is predicted to be almost entirely the result of immigration.

Whole extended families are arriving from other countries, bringing with them different cultural traditions and higher birthrates.

The most obvious impact of all this is the strain on infra-structure—housing, transport, healthcare, education. In every area, the welfare state is under pressure, much of it deriving from immigration.

David Goodhart has argued that the problem mass immigration poses for the Left is that it offends people's innate sense of fairness when newcomers are seen to be hoovering up benefits they have never contributed towards, and the welfare state is losing support as a result.

The economic benefits of immigration are hard to quantify, and much depends on which end of the telescope you are looking through. If you want to employ cheap labour, mass immigration is a good thing. If you are working in a low-paid trade or profession, it is a bad thing because it drives down pay.

The survival of the free society can be threatened by the presence within it of large numbers of people who do not share its most basic assumptions.

Immigration Endangers Values

But there is another issue that Julian Simon didn't have to face, as he died in 1998, before 9/11 [2001 terrorist attacks], and before we began to appreciate the extent to which the survival of the free society can be threatened by the presence within it of large numbers of people who do not share its most basic assumptions.

It is now becoming acceptable to say that not all immigrant groups behave in the same way. Some put more into the economy than they take out. Others don't.

Important as this distinction is, it pales into insignificance beside considerations such as belief in freedom of speech and worship, human rights and the freedom of the individual to make choices.

Even facing these new difficulties, I feel certain that Julian Simon would not have changed his position. He was so full of optimism, he never lost faith in the ability of the human spirit to triumph over any obstacle.

But as he was the most passionate believer in human freedom that I have ever known, I hope he can forgive me for changing mine.

Palestinian Population Growth Is a Myth Used to Intimidate Israel

Caroline B. Glick

Caroline B. Glick is an American-Israeli journalist. She is the deputy managing editor of The Jerusalem Post *and the senior fellow for Middle East Affairs of the Center for Security Policy in Washington, D.C. In the following viewpoint, Glick addresses the widespread belief that the Palestinian population is growing much more quickly than the Israeli Jewish population. Because of the belief that Palestinians will soon outnumber Jews, Glick says that the Israeli government has made important concessions to the Palestinians. However, Glick argues, the belief in rapid Palestinian growth is based on false data and propaganda. The Palestinian population is not, she says, growing faster than the Israeli Jewish population, and therefore Israel should not compromise or give in to Palestinian demands.*

As you read, consider the following questions:

1. The report "Demographic Indicators of the Palestinian Territory" claimed that Arabs would outnumber Jews west of the Jordan River in what year?

2. Is emigration from the Palestinian areas generally greater than or less than immigration into these areas?

Caroline B. Glick, "The Demographic Bomb Is a Dud," *The Jerusalem Post*, January 14, 2005. Reproduced by permission.

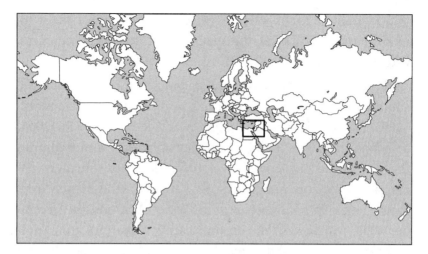

3. According to Glick, the actual number of Palestinians in Gaza, Judea, and Samaria is how much less than the figure formerly used?

It could be said in retrospect that the greatest single victory the PLO [Palestine Liberation Organization] has scored in its 46-year-old war with Israel was the publication of a single report in 1997. That report, "Demographic Indicators of the Palestinian Territory, 1997–2015," is based on a census carried out by the PA's [Palestinian Authority's] Central Bureau of Statistics (PCBS) in 1997. It projects that the Arab population west of the Jordan River will by 2015 outnumber the Jewish population.

These numbers were immediately adopted by such prominent Israeli demographers as the University of Haifa's Arnon Soffer and the Hebrew University's Sergio Della Pergola, who have both warned that by 2020 Jews will make up between 40 and 46 percent of the overall population of Israel and the territories. The Palestinian projections, which place the Arab population of Judea, Samaria and the Gaza Strip at 3.83 million and the Israeli Arab population at 1.33 million for a total of 5.16 million Arabs west of the Jordan River, put Israel with its 5.24 million Jews at the precipice of demographic parity with the Arabs.

Largely in reaction to these statistics, which were bandied about by everyone from politicians to diplomats to defense officials, Prime Minister Ariel Sharon decided a year ago [2004] to adopt the Labor Party's campaign platform and withdraw the IDF [Israeli Defense Force] from Gaza and northern Samaria and forcibly remove the Jews living in those areas from their homes. In his interview with Yediot Aharonot in December 2003, which was the curtain raiser for Sharon's announcement of his policy shift later that month, Vice Prime Minister Ehud Olmert said: "Above all hovers the cloud of demographics. It will come down on us not in the end of days, but in just another few years. We are approaching a point where more and more Palestinians will say: 'There is no place for two states between the Jordan and the sea. All we want is the right to vote.' The day they get it we will lose everything."

What if the doomsday scenarios we hear on a daily basis, arguing that Israel is about to be overrun by the Arab womb, are all based on fraudulent data?

Overestimated

But what if the numbers are wrong? What if the doomsday scenarios we hear on a daily basis, arguing that Israel is about to be overrun by the Arab womb, are all based on fraudulent data—part of an ingenious Palestinian plan to psychologically manipulate Israel into capitulating?

This week a team of American and Israeli researchers presented a study of the Palestinian population statistics at the American Enterprise Institute and the Heritage Foundation in Washington. . . .

All of the team's comparative analyses led to the conclusion that the Palestinian population forecasts upon which Israel is basing its current policy of withdrawal and uprooting of Israeli communities in the territories are faulty in the extreme.

The PCBS count includes the 230,000 Arab residents of Jerusalem. Yet these Arabs are already counted by the ICBS [Israeli Central Bureau of Statistics] as part of Israel's population, which means that they are counted twice.

The PCBS numbers also project Palestinian natural growth as 4 to 5 percent per year, among the highest in the world and significantly higher than the natural population growth of Egypt, Jordan, Lebanon and Syria. Yet Palestinian Ministry of Health records published annually since 1996 show that Palestinian natural growth rates in Judea, Samaria and Gaza average around 3 percent. In 2002, the Palestinian Ministry of Health retroactively raised its numbers and yet even the doctored figures never extended beyond 3.7 percent. The original data show a steady pattern of decrease in natural growth leading to a natural growth rate in 2003 of just 2.6 percent.

Indeed, the total fertility rate of Palestinian women has been trending downward in recent years. Palestinian women in Judea and Samaria averaged 4.1 children in 1999 and 3.4 in 2003. Palestinian women in Gaza averaged 5 children each in 1999 and 4.7 in 2003. The multi-year average of Israel's compound growth rate from 1990–2004 is 2.5 percent. And even as Israel's growth rate went down to 1.7 percent between 2000 and 2004, a similar decline occurred among Palestinians in Gaza, where growth decreased from 3.9 percent to 3.0 percent, and Palestinians in Judea and Samaria, where growth declined from 2.7 percent to 1.8 percent.

More Errors

The PCBS also projected a net population increase of 1.5 percent per year as a result of immigration from abroad. But the study's authors found that except for 1994, when the bulk of the Palestinian leadership and their families entered the areas from abroad, emigration from the Palestinian areas has outstripped immigration every year.

Aside from this, the PCBS numbers include some 200,000 Palestinians who live abroad. This fact was corroborated by an October 14 [2004] press release by the Palestinian Central Elections Commission which stated that "200,000 eligible voters are living abroad." The number of Palestinians living abroad constitutes 13 percent of the Palestinians counted in 1997 and forms the basis of the projections of that population's growth in spite of the fact that they don't live in the territories.

Indeed, the total fertility rate of Palestinian women has been trending downward in recent years.

The report also shows that while the Israeli Interior Ministry announced in November 2003 that in the preceding decade some 150,000 residents of the Palestinian Authority had legally moved to Israel (including Jerusalem), these 150,000 residents remain on the Palestinian population rolls. Parenthetically, this internal migration is largely responsible for the anomalous 3.1 percent annual growth in the Israeli Arab population. Absent this internal migration the Israeli Arab natural growth rate is 2.1%—that is, below the Israeli Jewish growth rate.

Not Outnumbered

The study presents three separate scenarios for calculating the actual Palestinian population in Judea, Samaria and the Gaza Strip. Its authors prove that the first scenario, based on the PCBS numbers, minus the double counted Jerusalem Arabs and minus the internal migrations, is not statistically plausible. Yet even this scenario places the Palestinian

Population of Israel and the Palestinian Territories, July 2008 Estimate

Israel has many more people than do the Palestinian territories of the West Bank and Gaza Strip.

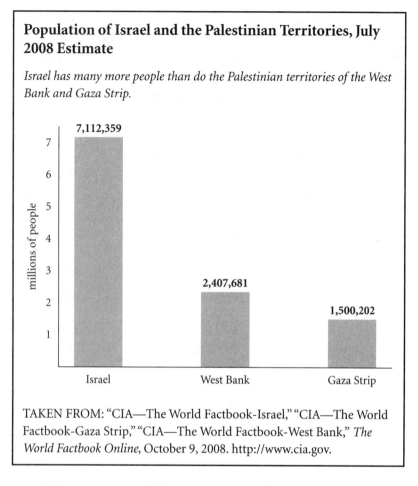

TAKEN FROM: "CIA—The World Factbook-Israel," "CIA—The World Factbook-Gaza Strip," "CIA—The World Factbook-West Bank," *The World Factbook Online*, October 9, 2008. http://www.cia.gov.

population at 3.06 million, or 770,000 less than the number that currently informs Israeli decision makers.

The average of the last two scenarios, which corrected for the Palestinians living abroad and were based on base populations comprised of ICBS Palestinian population survey projections from the 1990s and Palestinian voting records in 1996 and 2004, brought the final projected number of Palestinians in Gaza, Judea and Samaria to 2.42 million—nearly a third less than the 3.83 million figure currently being used.

The study, which has been accepted by prominent American demographers Dr. Nicholas Eberstadt and Murray Feshbach, shows that contrary to common wisdom, the Jewish majority west of the Jordan River has remained stable since 1967. In 1967 Jews made up 64.1 percent of the overall population and in 2004 they made up 59.5 percent. Inside Israel proper, including Jerusalem, Jews make up 80 percent of the population.

While reading the report, the inescapable sense is that something has gone very wrong within Israeli society. The numbers are so clear. The data have always been readily available. And yet, like bats attracted to the darkness of a cave, we preferred the manipulative lies of the PA to the truth.

Periodical Bibliography

Allianz Knowledge   "An Ocean Apart: European and U.S. Demographics Compared," July 18, 2008. www.knowledge.allianz.com.

Bitterlemons.org   "Demography and the Conflict," January 12, 2004. www.bitterlemons.org.

Barbara Crossette   "Population Estimates Fall as Poor Women Assert Control," *New York Times*, May 10, 2002.

The Economist   "Horrid History," May 22, 2008.

Philip Johnston   "Record Immigration Sees UK Population Soar," *Telegraph Online*, April 19, 2008. www.telegraph.co.uk.

Michele Kort   "Are U.S. Policies Killing Women?" *Ms.*, Winter 2008.

Brian Merchant   "The Latest Bold Initiative to Halt Population Growth: Daytime Soap Operas?" Treehugger.com, December 21, 2008. www.treehugger.com.

Jim Motavalli   "Now We Are Six," *E/The Environmental Magazine*, July/August 1999.

Richard Posner   "AIDS, Population, and Policy—Posner Response," The Becker-Posner Blog, December 27, 2004. www.becker-posner-blog.com.

Eamon Quinn   "Ireland Learns to Adapt to a Population Growth Spurt," *New York Times*, August 19, 2007.

John-Henry Western and Kathleen Gilbert   "Pope Against Population Control: 'Population Is Proving to Be an Asset, Not a Factor That Contributes to Poverty,'" LifeSiteNews.com, December 12, 2008. www.lifesitenews.com.

Jim Yardley   "China Sticking with One-Child Policy," *New York Times*, March 11, 2008.

For Further Discussion

Chapter 1

1. Janet Larsen warns that population growth must be slowed in nations like India and Nigeria or there may be a shortage of agricultural land and a food crisis. Paul Tuns, on the other hand, points out that there have been predictions of food crises in the past, and they have all been wrong, in part because improvements in agriculture have increased food production. Do you think we can rely on technological advances to prevent food scarcity in the future as has been done in the past? Explain why or why not.

2. George Monbiot argues that economic growth consumes more resources, and is more dangerous, than population growth. According to the articles by Antonio C. Abaya and Mestawet Taye Asfaw, have any economic development initiatives contributed to hunger in Ethiopia and/or the Philippines? Give specific examples.

Chapter 2

1. Imagine that an accident involving nuclear waste occurred on the Galapagos Islands. Radiation levels became so dangerous that all humans were forced to permanently abandon the island. Based on the essays by the Galapagos Conservancy Web site and by Patrick Burns, what effect would this disaster have on the wildlife? Would you expect rare species on the Galapagos to thrive or become extinct? Explain the reasoning behind your answer.

2. Khalid Md. Bahauddin says that "population growth is the primary threat to the world's environment." Based on the articles by WALHI (the Indonesian Forum for

Environment), Luke Sunner, and Gretchen Cook-Anderson, would you agree that population growth is the primary threat to Indonesian fisheries, Australian freshwater supplies, and the Asian environment? What other specific factors are also important?

Chapter 3

1. Tim Murray argues that Canada should stop aid to countries that do not lower their birthrates. According to Atanu Dey, would reducing incomes in poor nations cause an increase or decrease in population growth? Explain why.

2. Dietwald Claus claims that children do not contribute substantially to economic growth. If this argument is true, does it undermine or support *The Economist*'s prescription for population and economic growth in Europe? Explain why.

Chapter 4

1. Based on the article by Nie Jing-Bao, would more democracy and free speech be likely to increase or decrease the popularity of the one-child policy? Explain your answers.

2. Both Robert Whelan and Caroline B. Glick believe that a rapid growth in the Muslim population of their countries would be dangerous. Do you think it is intolerant or racist to express concern about the population growth of minority groups in a nation? Explain your reasoning.

Organizations to Contact

The editors have compiled the following list of organizations concerned with the issues debated in this book. The descriptions are derived from materials provided by the organizations. All have publications or information available for interested readers. The list was compiled on the date of publication of the present volume; the information provided here may change. Be aware that many organizations take several weeks or longer to respond to inquiries, so allow as much time as possible.

Alan Guttmacher Institute
125 Maiden Lane, 7th Floor, New York, NY   10038
(212) 248-1111 • fax: (212) 248-1951
e-mail: info@guttmacher.org
Web site: www.guttmacher.org

The Alan Guttmacher Institute is a sexual and reproductive health research group. It uses statistical data and research to protect and expand the reproductive choices for men and women, including birth control and safe and legal abortion. Its publications include the annual *Perspectives on Sexual and Reproductive Health*, the *International Family Planning Perspectives*, and *State Policies in Briefs*.

Center for Global Change Science (CGCS)
77 Massachusetts Avenue MIT 54-1312
Cambridge, MA   02139
(617) 253-4902 • fax: (617) 253-0354
e-mail: cgcs@mit.edu
Web site: http://web.mit.edu/cgcs

Center for Global Change Science (CGCS) at the Massachusetts Institute of Technology addresses long-standing scientific problems that impede accurate predictions for changes in global environment. The long-term goal of CGCS is to accurately predict environmental changes by utilizing scientific theory and observations to understand the basic processes and mechanisms controlling the global environment. The center publishes and distributes a Report Series of papers intended to communicate new results and provide reviews and commentaries on the subject of global climate change.

Center for Global Food Issues (CGFI)
PO Box 202, Churchville, VA   24421-0202
(540) 337-6354 • fax: (540) 337-8593
e-mail: cgfi@rica.net
Web site: www.cgfi.org

Center for Global Food Issues (CGFI) employs a global perspective in researching and analyzing the agricultural and environmental issues associated with farming. The Center promotes free trade and innovative farming technologies in addition to raising awareness about the effect of different farming methods on the environment. CGFI works to ensure sustainability of the global agriculture industry while keeping environmental conservation a central focus. Back issues of the center's publication *Global Food Quarterly* are available on its Web site, as are current reports on topics such as organic farming.

Friends of the Earth International
PO Box 19199, Amsterdam   1000 gd
   The Netherlands
31-206221369 • fax: 31-206392181
E-mail: foe@foe.org
Web site: www.foei.org

Friends of the Earth International is a global advocacy organization dedicated to protecting the planet from environmental degradation; preserving biological, cultural, and ethnic diversity; and empowering citizens to have an influential voice in decisions affecting the quality of their environment. It has a U.S. chapter and publishes numerous publications dealing with the environment. Recent publications include *How the World Bank's Energy Framework Sells the Climate and Poor People Short* and *The Tyranny of Free Trade*.

Intergovernmental Panel on Climate Change (IPCC)

C/O World Meteorological Organization

7bis Avenue de la Paix, C.P. 2300, Geneva 2   CH-1211
  Switzerland

41-227308208 • fax: 41-227308025

e-mail: IPCC-Sec@wmo.int

Web site: www.ipcc.ch

Recognizing the problem of potential global climate change,
the World Meteorological Organization and the United Nations Environment Programme established the Intergovernmental Panel on Climate Change (IPCC) in 1988. The IPCC's
role is to assess the scientific, social, and economic information relevant for the understanding of the risk of human-
induced climate change. The IPCC is currently publishing *Climate Change 2007*, which unequivocally blames human
activities for global warming.

International Organization for Migration (IOM)

17, Route des Morillons, Geneva 19   CH-1211
  Switzerland

41-227179111 • fax: 41-227986150

e-mail: hq@iom.int

Web site: http://www.iom.int

The goal of the International Organization for Migration
(IOM) is to help ensure the orderly and humane management
of migration, to promote international cooperation on migration issues, to assist in the search for practical solutions to migration problems, and to provide humanitarian assistance to
migrants in need, including refugees and internally displaced
people. IOM provides services for people who need international migration assistance, gives research and expert advice to
governments, and serves as a reference point for sharing information on migration issues. It publishes the journals *World
Migration Reports* and *International Migration*, the bulletin
"Migration," and numerous reports and publications.

Population Connection

2120 L Street NW, Suite 500, Washington, DC   20037
(202) 332-2200 • fax: (202) 332-2302
1-800-767-1956
e-mail: info@populationconnection.org
Web site: www.populationconnection.org

The goal of Population Connection (formerly Zero Population Growth) is to advocate for action to stabilize world population. Through government advocacy and the creation and distribution of educational materials, it supports removal of limitations on contraception and on access to abortion, and promotes increased aid for family planning services worldwide. The organization publishes a magazine about population called *The Reporter*.

Population Research Institute (PRI)

1190 Progress Drive, Suite 2D, PO Box 1559
Front Royal, VA   22630
(540) 622-5240 • fax: (540) 622-2728
e-mail: pri@pop.org
Web site: www.pop.org

The goal of the Population Research Institute (PRI) is to expose myths of overpopulation and to investigate human rights abuses committed in population control programs. PRI investigates and disseminates information about, and lobbies against, population control programs in the United States and abroad. Its publications include *Weekly Briefing* and the *PRI Review*, both available on its Web site.

UNESCO World Water Assessment Programme

7, place de Fontenoy, Paris 07 SP   75352
  France
33-(0)145681000 • fax: 33-(0)145685811
e-mail: wwap@unesco.org
Web site: www.unesco.org/water/wwap

The World Water Assessment Programme is part of the United Nations Educational, Scientific and Cultural Organization (UNESCO) and is designed to provide information related to global freshwater issues. Every three years, it publishes the United Nations World Water Development Report (WWDR), a comprehensive review that gives an overall picture of the state of the world's freshwater resources and aims to provide decision-makers with the tools to implement sustainable use of water.

United Nations Development Programme
One United Nations Plaza, New York, NY   10017
(212) 906-5000 • fax: (212) 906-5364
e-mail: mdg.support@undp.org
Web site: www.undp.org

In January 2007 the UN Millennium Project—eight global development goals adopted by 189 nations in 2000—was folded into the United Nations Development Programme, the UN network that helps governments address development problems such as democratic governance, poverty reduction, crisis prevention and recovery, energy and environment use, and HIV/AIDS. The most relevant resources can be found in the site's Millennium Development Goals and Poverty Reduction sections, which explain and track worldwide efforts to achieve Millennium Goal 1 (MDG1), the commitment to cut global poverty in half by 2015.

World Future Society
7910 Woodmont Avenue, Suite 450, Bethesda, MD   20814
(301) 656-8274 • fax: (301) 951-0394
e-mail: info@wfs.org
Web site: www.wfs.org

The World Future Society serves as a national clearinghouse for ideas and information about the future, including forecasts, recommendations, and alternative scenarios. These ideas help people to anticipate what may happen in coming years and to distinguish between possible, probable, and desired futures. The society publishes the bimonthly *Futurist* magazine and *Futures Research Quarterly*. On its Web site the society publishes lists of recommended books on issues concerning humanity's future, including energy, the environment, governance, health, and science and technology.

World Health Organization (WHO)
Avenue Appia 20, Geneva 27   1211
  Switzerland
41-(22)7912111 • fax: 41-(22)7913111
e-mail: info@who.int
Web site: www.who.int

The World Health Organization (WHO) is the United Nations specialized agency for health. Established in 1948, WHO seeks to promote the highest possible level of health for all people. Health is defined in WHO's Constitution as a state of complete physical, mental and social well-being, and not merely the absence of disease or infirmity. WHO is governed by 193 member countries through the World Health Assembly. WHO's Web site contains a library of reports and publications, as well as links to various world health journals and reports.

Worldwatch Institute
1776 Massachusetts Avenue NW
Washington, DC   20036-1904
(202) 452-1999 • fax: (202) 296-7365
e-mail: worldwatch@worldwatch.org
Web site: www.worldwatch.org

The Worldwatch Institute is a research organization that analyzes and calls attention to global problems, including environmental concerns such as the loss of cropland, forests, habitat, species, and water supplies. It compiles the annual State of the World anthology and publishes the bimonthly magazine *World Watch* and the *World Watch Paper Series*, which includes "Home Grown: The Case for Local Food in a Global Market" and "Underfed and Overfed: The Global Epidemic of Malnutrition."

Bibliography of Books

Maude Barlow — *Blue Covenant: The Global Water Crisis and the Coming Battle for the Right to Water*. Toronto, Canada: McClelland & Stewart, 2007.

Lester R. Brown, Gary T. Gardner, Brian Halwell — *Beyond Malthus: Nineteen Dimensions of the Population Challenge*. New York: W.W. Norton & Company, 1999.

Aine Collier — *The Humble Little Condom: A History*. Amherst, NY: Prometheus Books, 2007.

Paul Collier — *The Bottom Billion: Why the Poorest Countries Are Failing and What Can Be Done About It*. New York: Oxford University Press, 2007.

Matthew Connelly — *Fatal Misconception: The Struggle to Control World Population*. Cambridge, MA: Belknap Press, 2008.

Paul R. Ehrlich — *The Population Bomb*. New York: Ballantine Books, 1968.

Robert Engleman — *More: Population, Nature, and What Woman Want*. Washington, DC: Island Press, 2008.

John Firor and Judith E. Jacobsen — *The Crowded Greenhouse: Population, Climate Change, and Creating a Sustainable World*. Chicago, IL: R.R. Donnelly & Sons, 2002.

Thomas L. Friedman — *Hot, Flat, and Crowded: Why We Need a Green Revolution—and How It Can Renew America.* New York: Farrar, Straus, and Giroux, 2008.

Susan Greenhalgh and Edwin Wincklet — *Governing China's Population: From Leninist to Neoliberal Biopolitics.* Stanford, CA: Stanford University Press, 2005.

Lara M. Knudsen — *Reproductive Rights in a Global Context: South Africa, Uganda, Peru, Denmark, United States, Vietnam, Jordan.* Nashville, TN: Vanderbilt University Press, 2006.

Frances Moore Lappe, Joseph Collins, Peter Rosset, and Luis Esparza — *World Hunger: Twelve Myths.* 2nd ed. New York: Grove Press, 1998.

Ronald Demos Lee — *Global Population Aging and Its Economic Consequences.* Washington, DC: AEI Press, 2007.

Thomas Malthus — *An Essay on the Principle of Population.* Ed. Geoffrey Gilbert. New York: Oxford University Press, 1993.

Jeffrey K. McKee — *Sparing Nature: The Conflict Between Human Population Growth and Earth's Biodiversity.* Piscataway, NJ: Rutgers University Press, 2003.

Donella H. Meadows, Jorgen Randers, and Dennis L. Meadows — *Limits to Growth: The 30-Year Update*. White River Junction, VT: Chelsea Green Publishing Company, 2004.

Steven W. Mosher — *Population Control: Real Costs, Illusory Benefits*. New Brunswick, NJ: Transaction Publishers, 2008.

Craig A. Parsons and Timothy M. Smeeding, eds. — *Immigration and the Transformation of Europe*. New York: Cambridge University Press, 2006.

Warren C. Robinson and John A. Ross, eds. — *The Global Family Planning Revolution: Three Decades of Population Policies and Programs*. Washington, DC: The International Bank for Reconstruction and Development, 2007.

Jefrey D. Sachs — *Common Wealth: Economics for a Crowded Planet*. New York: Penguin Press, 2008.

Johanna Schoen — *Choice & Coercion: Birth Control, Sterilization, and Abortion in Public Health and Welfare*. Chapel Hill, NC: University of North Carolina Press, 2005.

Sheldon J. Segal — *Under the Banyan Tree: A Population Scientists's Odyssey*. New York: Oxford University Press, 2003.

Vandana Shiva — *Stolen Harvest: The Hijacking of the Global Food Supply*. Cambridge, MA: South End Press, 2000.

William Stanton *The Rapid Growth of Human Populations 1750–2000: Histories, Consequences, Issues, Nation by Nation.* Brentwood, UK: Multi-Science Publishing Co. Ltd., 2003.

Ben J. Wattenberg *Fewer: How the New Demography of Depopulation Will Shape Our Future.* Chicago, IL: Ivan R. Dee, 2004.

Alan Weisman *The World Without Us.* New York: Picador, 2007.

Index

Geographic headings and page numbers in **boldface** refer to viewpoints about that country or region.